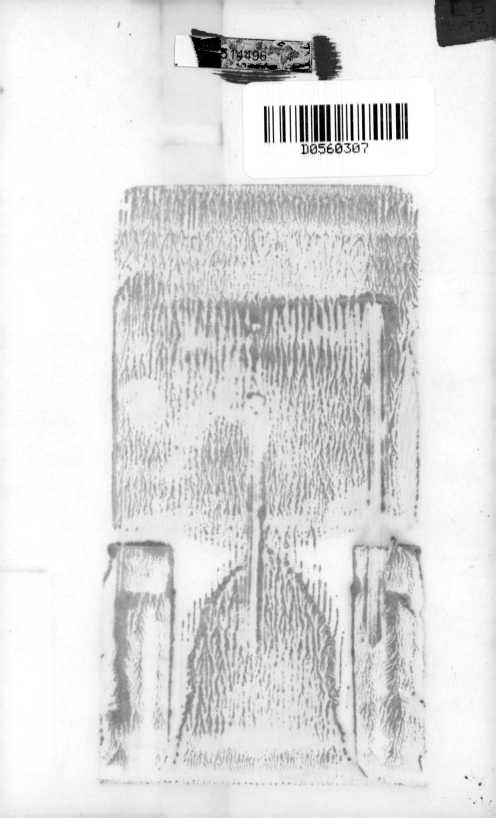

Shylock on the Stage

EDWIN BOOTH as SHYLOCK
*Walter Hampden Memorial Library
at The Players, New York.*

Shylock

on

the

Stage

BY

TOBY LELYVELD

THE PRESS OF
WESTERN RESERVE UNIVERSITY
CLEVELAND 6, OHIO

Designed by Harvey Satenstein

MANUFACTURED IN THE UNITED STATES OF AMERICA BY

BOOK CRAFTSMEN ASSOCIATES, INC., NEW YORK

In memory of

DAVY COIT

PREFACE

The purpose of this study is to trace the stage history of *The Merchant of Venice*. More specifically, it is an attempt to describe the manner in which Shylock has been characterized by actors who brought significant changes to the role on the English-speaking stage, from Shakespeare's own day to the present. It is hoped that this account will give some indication of the changes in social attitudes as they affected the development in successive presentations of Shakespeare's Jew. The many discussions of the text by literary critics will be considered here only insofar as they have had direct bearing on the stage performances.

Of the greatest dependability in determining the quality of stage presentations are the critical writings of those who witnessed them, the prompt-books, the memoirs of players and the journals of travellers. Playbills, records of theatre managers, log-books of theatres and annals of the stage have also provided rewarding sources of information. The libraries of Columbia University, Harvard University, the Folger Shakespeare Library, the Hiram Stead Collection and the Robinson Locke Collection of the New York Public Library, and The Players have been particularly helpful in making these materials available. Horace Howard Furness' New Variorum edition of *The Merchant of Venice* has served as a useful guide in determining the scope of this investigation.

This foreword would be incomplete without an expression of my indebtedness to Professor Maurice Jacques Valency for his guidance and encouragement, to Professors Oscar James Campbell and Alfred Harbage for their advice and interest, to the late Professors George C. D. Odell and Thomas Marc Parrott, Professor Arthur Colby Sprague and Dr. William Van Lennup for their informative conversations at the outset, to Mr. Willis Thornton for his aid in all the details of publication, and especially to my husband for his forbearance along the way.

Contents

Illustrations

Shylock on the Stage

CHAPTER I

In the Beginning

CONTENTIOUS discussion and a variety of interpretation surround the stage history of *The Merchant of Venice*. Shakespeare was primarily a showman. Among the many facets of his genius was the incomparable capacity to infuse life into stock characters. With conscious artistry, he created an eternally fascinating play out of his deep insight. The question of whether or not he intended his comedy to embody a thesis is related to a complex of psychological and sociological factors so intricate that it all but defies analysis.

The interest that surrounds the central character of *The Merchant of Venice* is no less intense today than it was in the sixteenth century. Shylock remains as vivid as Hamlet, but the evaluation of him as a character has a particular significance. The vastly differing audience responses to Shylock from the Elizabethan age to the twentieth century reveal the pace of the development of human understanding. The history of *The Merchant of Venice* gives us a glimpse of the changes in the theatre over a period of 360 years while the history of the playing of Shylock gives us the groundwork for some generalizations as to the shifts of social attitudes over the same period. At any rate, there is obviously something extraordinary in this play which has made it a consistent favorite with actors and public for so many centuries as a vehicle both for comedians and tragedians.

Shylock is, primarily, Shakespeare's conception of a Jew. Whatever was known of Jews in England during the years of their exile, came chiefly via the dubious route that ballads and the drama travelled. Popular ditties about the Wandering Jew and the numerous versions of the ballad that details the sad fate of little Hugh

3

of Lincoln at the hands of the "cruel" Jews were tearfully sung for many generations. In Chaucer's *The Prioress' Tale,* in which the story of Hugh of Lincoln is retold, in *Piers Plowman* and in John Gower's *Confessio Amantis,* there is further expression of the strong antipathy to Jews in England during this period. In medieval times, the stage-Jew was invaribly grotesque and evil. In the crucifixion pageants at York, the alleged brutalities and fiendish qualities of the Jews were emphasized. Later plays of the guilds struck the same anti-Jewish note. The Jews in the Corpus Christi pageants were characterized as inhuman and evil, and in *The Betraying of Christ* and *The Judgment Day,* they were made ridiculous in appearance, as well.

The contemporary background for these delineations is revealing. William the Conqueror had encouraged Jews to settle in England. They were granted a charter in the twelfth century and governed their own community according to Jewish law, which King John recognized as valid. But their sense of security was soon destroyed. In 1144, when a young boy disappeared in Norwich, there followed the accusation that the Jews had been responsible for his murder. The ensuing attack upon the Jewish settlement was the first in a long series of "ritual murder" incidents. Despite the protests of Pope Innocent IV, the accusations continued. During the reign of Henry II, however, the Jews were able to live under relatively favorable conditions, although they were still barred from the artisan guilds and prohibited from holding land.

Nevertheless, Jews were extremely useful in the economic scheme. No agency existed for money-lending, and since the Church forbade Christians to take interest, several Jews who had acquired wealth filled the gap in the economic life of England by becoming money-lenders. It was difficult to collect taxes. Powerful barons were constantly in need of money and they were willing to borrow and even to repay at interest. In this way, money accumulated in a number of Jewish coffers but these were drained periodically by the government which thus profited by ingenious means of indirect taxation. *The Jew of Malta* includes an example of this sort of taxation. The few Jews who became expert as bankers inevitably acquired power. Aaron of Lincoln became one of the most influential bankers of Europe.

A Jew could not bequeath his money to his heirs. He was regarded as a royal serf;[1] his funds, upon his death, were inherited by the king. Tax rates varied considerably. While Jews did not have the privileges of the Christian community, they were expected to support it. They were not exempt from the payment of church tithes. The Jews of England paid one-half of King Richard's 100,000 marks' ransom, while the entire city of London was assessed only 1,500 marks. In order to finance the Third Crusade, the Jews, as chattels of the crown, were taxed to the extent of one-fourth of their movable property, while the remainder of the population paid one-tenth. Although the Jews constituted only one-quarter of one percent of the total population of England in the twelfth century, they contributed eight percent of the total income of the treasury.[2]

In spite of all this, their position in England became increasingly precarious. Their expulsion from England was hastened by the rise of several Italian banking houses, to which England now gave its patronage. Jewish money-lenders began to lose their importance and their stay in England was now considered superfluous. In 1189, a deputation of Jews, bearing gifts to Richard I at the time of his coronation, was attacked by the mob and slaughtered. Other riots followed. In 1217, English Jews were made to wear the ignominious yellow badge. By this time, the word "Jew" had become a synonym for usurer, liar, rascal, cheat.

The Jews were exiled from England in 1290, in the reign of Edward I. Sixteen thousand of them left, taking with them their movable possessions. One-tenth of them fled to Flanders; the remainder sought refuge in France.[3] But a number of favored Jews un-

---

[1] "It should be known that all Jews, wheresoever in the realm they be, ought to be under the guard and protection of the King's liege. Nor ought any of them place himself under any rich man without the King's license; because the Jews themselves and all theirs belong to the King, and if any detain them or their money, let the King, if he will or can, ask it back as if it were his own." Cited by Joseph Jacobs, *The Jews of Angevin England*, London, 1893, p. 68.

[2] Salo Wittmayer Baron, *"A Social and Religious History of the Jews*, New York, 1937, vol. II, p. 18.

[3] According to one historian, many of the 16,000 Jews who left, perished on the way. Some 2000 went to Flanders, Brabant and Guelderland. Others went to the borderland between Flanders and France. Elkan Nathan Adler, *London*, Philadelphia, 1930, p. 62.

doubtedly remained even after the expulsion was ordered. To their number were added, in time, the many Jewish refugees who fled to London from Spain during the Inquisition. Some historians are of the opinion that there was a considerable number of Jewish descendants in London in Shakespeare's day, since special arrangements had to be made to accommodate them in the chapels of the Spanish and Portuguese embassies.[4] They existed as *Marranos,* or crypto-Jews, who outwardly professed their adherence to Christianity but who secretly worshipped as Jews.[5] Those who came to England in Elizabeth's time lived in greater safety there than had their forebears in Spain.[6]

Certain group characteristics that might generally be termed "Jewish" must have been apparent to the keen observer in Shakespeare's day. But a close acquaintance with the sectarian practices of Jews could not have been possible for outsiders at a time when those practices were outlawed. England's archives were well-kept; there is no record of any disaffection among these pseudo-Christians. To all intents, there were no longer any Jews in England.

Thus, when Shakespeare presented *The Merchant of Venice,* Shylock's outrageous behavior came as no shock to the Elizabethans. They sided with the Christians in the play, whose terms of opprobrium for Shylock reflected the popular attitude. It was natural for them to accept the sentence that compelled Shylock to turn Christian. They hated his religion as much as they did that of a Jesuit or a Turk.

The execution of Rodrigo Lopez, Portuguese-Jewish physician to Queen Elizabeth, in 1594, very likely provided Shakespeare with a springboard for his play. Lopez, who had been physician to the Earl of Leicester, Burbage's patron, had been implicated in a series of court intrigues that stemmed from a long-standing enmity between the physician and the Earl of Essex. Although later historians have found only inconclusive evidence of his guilt in plotting against the life of the queen, the Elizabethans had nothing but loathing for the

---

[4] Salo Wittmayer Baron, *The Jewish Community,* Philadelphia, 1942, vol. I, p. 255.

[5] Lucien Wolf, with the aid of Inquisition records, concludes that almost one hundred Jews resided in England during Elizabeth's reign. Presidential Address to the Jewish Historical Society of England, Manchester, November 21, 1926.

[6] Adler, *op. cit.,* p. 80.

proselytized Jew, and they rejoiced at his death. If any parallel could be drawn between Lopez and Shylock, the Elizabethans would have been quick to recognize it. Hatred of the Jews in the sixteenth century is not a matter of conjecture. Reviling the Jew was part of the social convention of Shakespeare's day.

Christopher Marlowe's characterization of Barabas in *The Jew of Malta*[7] was considered so appropriate, in fact, that it was presented twice within ten days following Lopez' hanging.[8] Barabas is unrelievedly and preposterously villainous, and his role suffers from a lack of nuance. The Elizabethans jeered at his excesses and hooted at the moment of his fierce and shrieking death. Apparently, as the stage representative of the Jews, he was perennially interesting.

It is largely a matter of guesswork as to whether it was Richard Burbage or Will Kempe who first played Shylock. There are ample grounds for suspecting that either actor could have played the role to the complete satisfaction of an Elizabethan audience. But since Kempe played comedy, and there is no evidence that Shylock was played as a comic character in Shakespeare's day, the probability is considerable that Burbage played the part. Whether or not Shylock was played seriously, there can be no doubt that whoever essayed the role gave it the unsympathetic reading that the sixteenth-century playgoer had come to expect.

For a great many years, writers had referred with confidence to the "red-haired Jew", in describing the appearance of the actor who played Shylock in Shakespeare's day. We know now that the phrase originates in a Collier forgery.[9] The occasion for the imposture was a poem entitled *A Funeral Elegy on the Death of the Famous Actor, Richard Burbage* that Collier claimed to have found in manuscript. Related to Shylock are the lines:

> Heart-broken Philaster, and Amintas too,
> Are lost forever; with the red-hair'd Jew,
> Who sought the bankrupt merchant's pound of flesh,
> By woman-lawyer caught in his own mesh

[7] Written *circa* 1590; it was not printed until 1594. Its first recorded stage presentation was in the week of February 26, 1592.

[8] During the weeks of June 8 and 15, 1594, at Newington Butts. These were succeeded by performances at The Rose Theatre during the weeks of June 27, July 6 and 13.

[9] John Payne Collier, literary and dramatic critic, whose numerous interesting "discoveries" in Elizabethan records were later found to be his own manuscript additions.

Yet, the failure of this interesting bit of "evidence" to establish the original color of Shylock's beard, does not, of course, indicate that Shylock's beard was not red. The chances are that it was, for Edmund Kean's first use of a black beard in 1814, created such a stir that we are led to believe that it was a drastic departure from the conventional practice of the actors who played Shylock.

Many reasons have been advanced for the use of a red beard. Some writers believe that dressing Shylock in this manner was an attempt to make the character mirror Judas Iscariot, whose beard was traditionally red. Others believe that this make-up was an imitation of Lopez' appearance. The argument that it reflected the fashion of the day seems a bit tenuous, since there would have been no point in making Shylock a fashionable figure.

Supposedly, the original Shylock rejoiced also in the possession of an artificial nose of stately proportions. Tradition has it that actors who played Barabas were adorned with such an appendage, although the basis for the assumption lies only in a fleeting reference to the Jew's nose by Ithamore in Marlowe's play.[10] Nevertheless, in time, a false nose became standard equipment with actors who played stage-Jews. The use of a false nose was part of the vast stock of word-of-mouth tradition in which the theatre abounds. Repeated with sufficient frequency, it soon became accepted as incontrovertible fact.

Shylock's resemblance to Pantalone of the *Commedia dell' Arte* is a striking one. In physical appearance, mannerisms and the situations in which he is placed, Shylock is so like his Italian prototype that his characterization, at least superficially, presents no new aspects save that of its Jewishness. Pantalone is a Venetian tradesman. He is traditionally avaricious and, of course, a comic mask. The Elizabethans knew him well. A drawing of Pantalone, in 1601, shows a beard, a false nose, a hat, a cloak worn over the conventional Venetian costume. He has a knife in his belt.[11] The caption might read, convincingly, "Shylock". If Pantalone is a source for Shakespeare's Shylock, this is another proof of the writer's genius. In transforming a stock character of comedy into a striking tragic character Shakespeare certainly exhibits astonishing virtuosity.

---

[10] Act II, Scene iii, line 178.

[11] Reproduced in a brochure by John Robert Moore, *Pantaloon as Shylock,* *Boston Public Library Quarterly,* July, 1949.

The title-page of the First Quarto edition shows us where the emphasis of the play was placed:

THE EXCELLENT History of *The Merchant of Venice*. With the extreme cruelty of Shylocke the Jew towards the saide Merchant, in cutting a just pound of his flesh, And the obtaining of Portia, by the choice of three Caskets.

The First Folio calls the play "The Comicall Historie" and appends to the title the caption: "As it has beene divers times acted by the Lord Chamberlaine his Servants." It was the iniquities of Shylock that were featured, and since these first editions of the play were undoubtedly printed from actors' copies, it is obvious what the chief appeal of the play was considered to be from its earliest time.

The Merchant of Venice is developed boldly, swiftly and dramatically. The number of lines a character has to speak usually is a trustworthy indication of his relative importance; it is interesting to note Shylock's economy of speech. He appears in only five of a total of twenty scenes. In all, only thirty considerable speeches are allotted to him. Yet, in this comparatively scanty part there is extraordinary opportunity for an actor to display the range of his talents, and the greatest actors have sought the role.

The early stage history of *The Merchant of Venice* is meager. The first reference to a stage presentation is to be found in a list, probably forged, but undoubtedly based on a genuine document used by Malone, of the plays given at Court in 1604-5.[12] According to this, *The Merchant of Venice* was witnessed by James I in a production by the King's Men on February 10, 1605, and the king admired it sufficiently to order its reshowing two days later. Unhappily, the Court Revels Account tells us nothing more of that command performance at Whitehall by "Shaxberd". The play, of course, could not have been new at this time. The earliest probable date we can set for it is 1594—the year of Lopez' hanging. Bearing in mind the steady demand for new additions to the dramatic repertory of the day, it is not likely that *The Merchant of Venice* languished for want of production between the years of its completion and the 1605 entry, but we have nothing with which to document its history from that date to the closing of the theatres by the Puritans in 1642.

The conjecture that the play produced at the Rose Theatre in

[12] Edmond Malone, *An Historical Account of the English Stage,* London, 1793 (not paginated).

1594 and recorded in Henslowe's diary as *A Venyson Comedy*[13] was *The Merchant of Venice* will hardly bear close scrutiny. Shakespeare, as head of the Lord Chamberlain's Men, was performing regularly with Burbage and Kempe in that year. It was Edward Alleyn and the Admiral's Men who were then acting at the Rose. A number of earlier plays with Jewish characters had already found public favor. Gerontus, in *The Three Ladies of London*, the only virtuous stage-Jew in the drama of this period, Marlowe's murderous Barabas, and Abraham, the poisoner, in Robert Green's *Selimus*, were Shylock's dramatic forebears. There is every reason to believe that Shakespeare would have seized the earliest opportunity to dramatize a Jewish character. Francis Meres mentions *The Merchant of Venice* in 1598—the very year that the play was registered at Stationer's Hall. It is improbable that Shakespeare's play would have been included in a reference to the playwright's excellence in comedy and tragedy had it not first been theatrically tested and found to be praiseworthy. The appearance of John Day's *The Travels of Three English Brothers* in 1607, with its travesty on Shylock in the character of Zariph, indicates not only a continuing interest in Shakespeare's Jew, but also a considerable familiarity with him.

When the theatres were reopened in 1660, Shakespeare suffered at least a partial eclipse. Any attempts to revive his work came by way of questionable alterations of his plays by clumsy adapters. Their "improvements" often approached vandalism; nevertheless, they found public favor. What the Restoration theatregoer considered Shakespearean was, in reality, a combination of song and spectacle superimposed upon the tragedies as well as on the comedies, in such a way to make them approximate masques and operas. Davenant, Tate, Cibber and Granville were among the worst offenders.

As habitual a playgoer as Samuel Pepys was quite unaware of Shakespeare's art. While he witnessed forty-one performances of Shakespeare's plays in his 351 recorded visits to the theatre, his less than moderate praise of the plays indicates that their quality eluded him. He tells in his *Diary* that many of them were "insipid" and "ridiculous". Doubtless, what he saw was of this nature. We find him chiefly susceptible to the music and to the women who were,

---

[13] Philip Henslowe's *Diary*, London, 1845, p. 40.

for the first time, appearing on the stage, and this, with his admiration of the acting of Thomas Betterton, foremost actor of his day, suggests the character of the performances. He does not mention *The Merchant of Venice,* and judging by the general absence of reference to the play at this time, it is probable that he never saw it. Betterton never played Shylock. The distinction of botching *The Merchant of Venice* belongs solely to Granville, who will be considered later.

In 1664, there was published in a collection called *The Royal Arbor of Loyal Poesie,* a ballad entitled *The Forfeiture,* by Thomas Jordan. The ballad relates the story of the pound of flesh in thirteen eight-line verses. Its description of Shylock calls to mind the earlier pictures of Pantalone:

> His beard was red; his face was made
> Not much unlike a witches.
> His habit was a Jewish gown
> That would defend all weather;
> His chin turn'd up, his nose hung down,
> And both ends met together.

Portia is replaced by Jessica, as the young judge, and to abridge the story further, the merchant, whose life she saves, is her suitor. The doggerel concludes:

> I wish such Jews may never come
> To England, nor to London.

From the appearance of *The Forfeiture* at this date, Collier concludes that *The Merchant of Venice* had been virtually forgotten after Burbage's death in 1619.[14]

At this time, a Jew was still considered an oddity in London. There were only 150 of them living in all of England in the middle of the seventeenth century, and their residence there, for all of Charles II's favorable attitude in recognition of the financial aid that the Jews of Holland had given him, was not generally regarded with cordiality. Exclusive of this number were the descendants of the *Marranos* of Shakespeare's day. These were now considered members of the Christian community. There was, however, during Cromwell's reign, a modicum of religious freedom for the Jews. In 1655, Menasseh ben Israel, an eminent rabbi, came from Holland to speak to Parliament in behalf of the readmission of Jews to

---

[14] *Illustrations of Old English Literature,* London, 1866, vol. III, pp. 133 ff.

England. Some years before, Menasseh had addressed a similar petition to Parliament. Cromwell, aware of the usefulness of the Jews in promoting trade, had encouraged the rabbi in his mission.

There were, in addition to economic considerations, ample religious grounds for the Puritans to welcome the resettlement of the Jews. The Puritans believed that only when Jews dwelled in every land would the Messianic Age dawn.[15] Converting Jews to Christianity was, according to their view, a sacred obligation, and offering hospitality to the Jews would hasten the practice of that duty. The less devout class of merchants, on the other hand, feared that their economic status would be endangered by the presence of the Jews, and strongly opposed their entry.

Menasseh's stay in England was prolonged, and at the time of his death in 1657, the Jews were in no better or worse state than they had been in Elizabeth's day. Nevertheless, Menasseh's presence had helped to establish the opinion that there was no legal basis for the Jews' banishment. Despite the immediate failure of general Jewish immigration, individual applicants were approved and the Jewish community was gradually, although precariously, re-established. But naturalization at this time was out of the question. A number of the neo-Christians, encouraged by the trend toward cordiality, publicly professed their adherence to Judaism and the first Jewish congregation since 1290 was established in London in 1663.[16] We recall the fascination that the new synagogue had for non-Jews, in Pepys' account of his visit there. It had become one of London's curiosities:

> After dinner my wife and I, by Mr. Rawlinson's conduct, to the Jewish Synagogue; where the men and boys in their vayles, and the women behind a lattice out of sight; and some things stand up, which I believe is their Law, in a press, to which all coming in do bow; and in the putting on their vayles do say something, to which the others that hear

---

[15] Illustrative of this view is the following excerpt of a letter sent by Major General Whalley to Mr. Secretary Thurloe: ". . . It seems to me there are divine reasons . . . for their admission . . . where wee both pray for theyre conversion, and believe it shall be, I know not why wee should deny the meanes. . . ." Cited by Cecil Roth, *A Life of Menasseh Ben Israel*, Philadelphia, 1934, p. 238.

[16] Adler cites a contemporary list for this period, indicating, in fact, two Synagogues; one for the Sephardim in Creechurch Lane, and one for the German Jews in Great St. Helens. *London*, p. 103.

the priest do cry, Amen, and the party do cry, Amen, and the party do kiss his vayle. Their service all in a singing way, and in Hebrew. And anon their Laws that they take out of the press are carried by several men, four or five several burthens in all, and they do relieve one another; and whether it is that every one desires to have the carrying of it, thus they carried it round about the room while such a service is singing. And in the end they had a prayer for the King, in which they pronounced his name in Portugall; but the prayer, like the rest, in Hebrew. But, Lord! to see the disorder, laughing, sporting, and no attention, but confusion in all their service, more like brutes than people knowing the true God, would make a man foreswear ever seeing them more; and indeed I never did see so much, or could have imagined there had been any religion in the whole world, so absurdly performed as this.[17]

What Pepys records is the observance of the Hakafoth portion, the joyous procession in the Simchath Torah[18] service. This holiday, concluding the harvest festival, is characterized by a spirit of gaiety on the completion of the annual cycle of readings of the Pentateuch and the beginning of the new cycle, which follows immediately, with the reading of the opening chapters of Genesis. As the usual restraints are not observed on this holiday, it is quite understandable that the scene of rejoicing might have astonished the impressionable Mr. Pepys.

Despite the good-will of Charles II, the faction that opposed any form of emancipation for Jews grew in strength. In 1673, the Jewish elders of London were indicted by the London Grand Jury for conducting religious services contrary to the Conventicle Act of 1664.[19] Charles promptly ordered the legal proceedings halted. But this intercession in their favor brought the Jewish community no closer to a legal recognition of their rights. In 1685, when Parliament contested the power of the crown in such matters, it found in James II the same tolerant attitude toward Jewish rights that his brother had exhibited. The anti-Jewish faction of the House of Commons

---

[17] Samuel Pepys' Diary, London, 1943, vol. I, p. 414.

[18] "Rejoicing in the Torah." Torah (lit.: teaching) is the word commonly applied to the scroll containing the first five books of the Bible.

[19] This law forbade the meeting of more than five persons for worship, except in church. Thus, a Minyan (the presence of ten men for a worship service) was illegal.

continued its campaign. Later that year forty-eight Jews were charged with recusancy and fined £20 a month for not attending church services, but the king enjoined further proceedings against them:

> His Majesty's intention being that they should not be troubled on this account, but quietly enjoy the free exercise of their religion, whilst they behave themselves dutifully and obediently to his government.

Nor did the Protestant Toleration Act of 1688, under William and Mary come any closer to legalizing the position of the Jews. Their status remained ambiguous. Neither the Catholics nor the Unitarians fared any better at this time.[20] An interesting sidelight, however, is to be found in the gift that Queen Anne made, in 1702, of a main beam for the Bevis Marks Synagogue as a special mark of her favor.

The Merchant of Venice has no history during the Restoration period. Although the title is included in a long list published for 1668-69, of the plays alloted to Thomas Killigrew,[21] our interest in the stage history of the play is not satisfied until the opening of the eighteenth century. The years that followed the re-opening of the theatres proved how devastating censorship can be. In 1701, Granville brought out his version of *The Merchant of Venice*. If we find it difficult to justify the applause for *The Jew of Venice*, as it was renamed, it is a fact that the playgoers who hailed it knew the play in no other form. George Granville, who became in time Lord Lansdowne, was thirty three years old when he foisted his adaptation upon his public. At this time, the Fourth Folio was in its sixteenth year. Nicholas Rowe's first edition of Shakespeare's works was not to be issued until eight years later. When Rowe wrote, in 1709, that he believed that Shakespeare intended Shylock to be a tragic character, he was undoubtedly thinking of the shabby treatment the money-lender received in *The Jew of Venice*:

> . . . tho we have seen the Play Receiv'd and Acted as a Comedy, and the Part of the *Jew* perform'd by an Excellent Comedian. . . .[22]

---

[20] Baron, *The Jewish Community,* Vol. I, p. 255 ff.

[21] Allardyce Nicoll, *A History of Restoration Drama,* 1660-1700, Cambridge, 1928, p. 162.

[22] Nicholas Rowe, *Some Accounts of the Life of Mr. William Shakespear,* in *Shakespearean Criticism* edited by D. Nichol Smith, Oxford, 1930, p. 31.

Granville's adaptation is an extraordinary piece of work. The ghost of Shakespeare appears in the Prologue, written by Bevill Higgons, and declares modestly:

> These Scenes in their rough Native Dress were mine;
> But now improv'd with nobler Lustre shine;
> The first rude Sketches Shakespear's Pencil drew,
> But all the shining Master-stroaks are new.
> This Play, ye Critiks, shall your Fury stand,
> Adorn'd and rescu'd by a faultless Hand. . . .

Granville interpolates scenes, omits characters, improvises dramatic incidents, jumbles Shakespeare's poetry with his own doggerel. So indiscriminating is his tampering, that the resultant perversion has only the merest resemblance to its original.

The theme of the Shylock plot of Granville's play is found in a topical reference in the Prologue:

> Today we punish a Stock-jobbing Jew.
> A Piece of Justice, terrible and strange;
> Which, if persued, would make a thin Exchange. . . .

At this time, in pursuance of a statute passed in 1697, the number of Jews on the London stock-exchange was limited by law to twelve.[23] The extension of even this privilege excited a good deal of dissatisfaction in financial circles, and Granville seized the opportunity to contemporize Shylock by the reference. Stock-jobbing, by the current definition, meant a "sharp, cunning, cheating Trade of Buying and Selling Shares of Stock."[24] The timely allusion might well have done something to bring the theme up to date, but nothing could have been more remote in establishing a mood of appreciation for Shakespeare's work.

Shakespeare, we will recall, had often resorted to the use of prose. Granville converted the prose passages into verse through the simple method of breaking up the speeches into lines of fairly equal length. Thus regularized, Shylock's famous speech looks strange:

> To bait Fish withal; if it will feed nothing else it
> Will feed my Revenge: Thou hast disgrac'd me,
> Hinder'd me half a Million; laught at my losses;
> Repin'd at my Gains; scorned my Nation;
> Thwarted my Bargains; cool'd my friends,
> Enflam'd my Enemies; and what's the Reason? . . .

---

[23] This number was included in the total of one hundred brokers admitted to practice by the Corporation of London.

[24] J. H. Wilson, Philological Quarterly, XIII (1934), pp. 1-15.

Morocco, Arragon, the Gobbos, Salarino, Salanio and Tubal are all omitted, perhaps in the interest of Granville's idea of unity and decorum. The revised title of the play is misleading; Shylock, in the title-role, has fewer lines than any other major character in this version. He appears in only four scenes and his speeches are noticeably curtailed. We find Granville's Shylock in Act I, Scene 3, in which the bargain is made; in Act II, Scene 3, where he feasts with Bassanio, Antonio and Gratiano; in Act III, Scene 3, where he appears with Antonio and the gaoler; and in the Trial Scene.

Granville's plan seems to have been to make the play a romantic comedy revolving about Bassanio. Only by de-emphasizing the Shylock plot and by disregarding a number of Shakespeare's other characters, could he effect this change. Betterton, no longer young, but still the leading man at Lincoln's Inn Fields, played Bassanio. Charles II had given his coronation robes to the actor. The role of Bassanio did not call for such spendid attire, and the spectators, accustomed to seeing Betterton in the king's finery, must have been impressed with the lesser costume with which he undoubtedly dressed this part. Anna Bracegirdle played Portia.

While Granville follows the general lines of the plot of *The Merchant of Venice,* his departures from Shakespeare's text are conspicuous. Rowe wrote in his preface to Shakespeare's works that only two passages deserve particular notice: Portia's "quality of mercy" speech and the reference to music in Act V. Here again, he may have been influenced by the only existing stage version of his time. Granville's Shylock grows anatomically expansive in discussing the pound of flesh with Antonio:

> Let me see, What think you of your Nose,
> Or of an Eye — or of — a pound of Flesh
> To be cut off, and taken from what Part
> Of your Body — I shall think fit to name,
> Thou art too portly, Christian!
> Too much pamper'd — What say you then
> To such a merry Bond?

Antonio appears at the scene of Jessica's flight, to hasten the men to a banquet. Gratiano explains that "Matters of State" have detained them; these being rape and robbery. Granville is most ambitious in the banquet scene that he invents. Shylock attends, but he sits apart from the Christians. While they toast Friendship, Love and Health,

Shylock drinks to Money, his mistress, to "interest upon interest." Lorenzo's lines about music from Act V of Shakespeare's play are interpolated here: It is Bassanio who says:

> The reason is, your spirits are attentive.
>
> . . . .
> The man that hath no music in himself,
> Nor is not mov'd with concord of sweet sounds,
> Is fit for treasons, strategems, and spoils;
>
> . . . .
> Let no such man be trusted. . . .

The music that accompanies this scene ushers in an interminable masque of Peleus and Thetis. The jailer scene, frequently deleted in later Shakespearean productions, but included by Granville, combines Shylock's speeches from Act III, Scene 1 of Shakespeare and incorporates the speech, "To bait fish withal," in the form cited above. This speech Shylock delivers directly to Antonio. A few additional variations tempt Granville. "The villainy you teach me ..." becomes "The Charity you practice I will Imitate . . . but I will improve by the Instruction." Immediately following is Shylock's speech about Leah's ring, his daughter and his ducats, and again, it is Antonio who hears these outpourings.

In the trial scene, even Portia's speech, "The quality of mercy," is "improved":

> The Quality of Mercy is not strain'd;
> It drops as does the gentle Dew from Heav'n
> Upon the Place beneath: It is twice blest,
> It blesses him that gives and him that takes
> Tis mightiest in the mightiest: It becomes
> The Crown'd Monarch, better than his Crown
> It is the first of sacred Attributes,
> And Earthly Power does then seem most Divine,
> When Mercy seasons Justice . . .

Antonio instructs Shylock to cut deep enough, "for I would have my Heart seen by My Friend." Bassanio interposes here and offers himself for sacrifice: "Take every piece of mine, and tear it off with Pincers." Shylock's response to Portia's dictum about shedding one drop of blood is expressed in a single "Humph!" Gratiano's jibes at Shylock are multiplied with many interpolated lines, in order to increase their comic effect. In Act V, Portia presents proof of her masquerade as a lawyer, by giving Jessica a deed signed by Shylock.

The intended humor of Granville's version is not as apparent in the reading as is its marked vulgarity. It may be, of course, as Odell surmises, that what seemed amusing to audiences at that time was made evident by the action and the appearance of Shylock.[25] We have no means of evaluating such a conjecture; all we know is that the play was offered and accepted as a comedy. We gather from the reputations of the actors who were involved in this parody that they probably worked uninhibitedly at the task of devastating whatever charm and nobility was left in Shakespeare's play.

From the casting of the play, it may, for example, be inferred that it was executed in the vein of the lowest comedy. Thomas Doggett, who had been before the public since 1691, and was the outstanding comedian of his day, was cast as Shylock in the 1701 production. Shylock was not Doggett's first Jewish role. He had played Sancho, an apostate Jew, in Dryden's *Love Triumphant* some years before. John Downes, who had served as prompter at Lincoln's Inn Fields for many years, wrote of Doggett in his *Roscius Anglicanus*[26] ... with the names of the most taking plays":

> On the Stage he's very aspectabund, wearing a Farce in his Face; his Thoughts deliberately framing his utterance congruous to his looks: He is the only Comic Original now extant; Witness, *Ben, Solon, Nikin, The Jew of Venice* &c.

Cibber was a personal friend and at one time a partner of Doggett. Following a law-suit, which left both men on bad terms, Cibber, nevertheless, gave testimony to Doggett's ability:

> In dressing a character to the greatest exactness, he was remarkably skilful; the least article of whatever habit he wore seem'd in some degree to speak and mark the different humour he presented. . . . He could be extremely ridiculous, without stepping into the least impropriety to make him so. His greatest success was in characters of lower life. . . .[27]

While these comments convey no information as to Doggett's performance of Shylock, they imply how thoroughly he must have developed his comic characterization. As Cibber indicates, Doggett was a master of comic roles and his Shylock undoubtedly served among

---

[25] George C. D. Odell, *Shakespeare from Betterton to Irving*, New York, 1920, vol. I, p. 79.

[26] London, 1789, p. 69.

[27] Colley Cibber, *An Apology for His Life*, London, 1938, p. 252.

the best illustrations of that talent. *The Jew of Venice* was only moderately popular in the years preceding Doggett's death in 1721, Griffin occasionally taking over the role at Lincoln's Inn Fields.[28] Griffin was a competent comedian, and he continued in the tradition that had been established by Doggett. Only one or two performances a season featured Shylock in the ensuing years.[29] Nevertheless, by 1736 *The Jew of Venice* had gone through six published editions.

Pope's admiration of Shakespeare's works, of which his edition of the plays in 1725 gives evidence, apparently brought no influence to bear on their stage presentation. In the years following Theobald's admirable 1733 edition of the plays, audiences continued to be as innocent of any acquaintance with Shakespeare's *The Merchant of Venice* as they had been in 1701, but Granville's version gained renewed popularity at the newly-opened Covent Garden. Any relationship that may have existed between the reading and the playgoing public was entirely fortuitous. Then, as now, scholarship bred scholarship and was not nurtured on popular support.

This was the state of affairs that existed until Charles Macklin presented a characterization of Shylock almost a decade later, resulting, not in ripples of interest that he had hopefully anticipated, but in a veritable storm of controversy.

---

[28] Charles Beecher Hogan, *Shakespeare in the Theatre, 1701-1800*, Oxford, 1952, p. 309.

[29] Allardyce Nicoll, *A History of Early Eighteenth Century Drama*, 1700-1750, Cambridge, 1925, p. 134.

CHARLES MACKLIN as SHYLOCK
*Hiram Stead Collection
of the New York Public Library*

CHAPTER II

Charles Macklin

WHEN Charles Macklin announced his intention to depart from the comic tradition that had been established by way of the Granville version of *The Merchant of Venice,* the play had been off the boards for more than two years. He encountered nothing but derision and discouragement on the part of his colleagues at the Drury Lane. They believed that a serious treatment of Shylock would be only an arrogant and presumptuous display. But Macklin did not permit himself to be dissuaded. After deliberately underacting at rehearsals, in order to avoid the criticism of his associates, he presented a characterization of Shylock on February 14, 1741 that was to become the precursor of an interpretation for many of the great tragedians who were to undertake the role.

We have no direct information as to the acting version that Macklin used. No Macklin prompt-book of the play is extant. It may be assumed with some certainty, however, that the Bell edition of 1774 follows his text in most essentials. From the Bell edition we conclude that Macklin cut lines in many scenes. In Act I of the Bell version, Portia's jibes at the English and the Scotch are deleted. Francis Gentleman's inclusion of footnotes, however, compensates for the omissions throughout the edition.[1] Bell opens Act II with the Gobbo scene, ignoring Morocco and later, Arragon. Macklin retained both suitors. Tubal had been overlooked by Granville, but he served as such an effective foil for Shylock that he was now restored to the *dramatis personae.* The trial scene was kept almost intact; only five important lines are excised from it. Act V was entirely faithful to Shakespeare.

---

[1] Odell pays tribute to Gentleman's delicate literary conscience for the inclusion of footnotes. *Shakespeare from Betterton to Irving,* New York, 1920, Vol. II, p. 25.

From 1741, when David Garrick first began to edit Shakespeare's plays, there was an appreciable interest in the frequency of their presentation. *The Merchant of Venice* was performed twenty times during the first three months of Macklin's success. Of the comedies, during a later, more typical season at the Drury Lane, *The Merchant of Venice* ran three nights and *Twelfth Night* ran two.[2] This seems to be an inconsequential number of performances, but it must be remembered that the repertory system during this period precluded extended runs. *The Merchant of Venice* apparently, was a favored play and could be counted on to bring in good grosses. It was doubtless for this reason that it was so frequently selected for benefit performances during this period.[3]

It is interesting to note that Garrick's is the one great name in the theatre that is not associated with the Shylock role. He may have felt that he was unsuited for the part, for indeed his "finished" quality of acting could hardly have been suited to a role that was far from polished or heroic. Moreover, Garrick had engaged in heated controversy with Macklin over Fleetwood's management of the Drury Lane shortly before Lacy took it over, and although both men finally emerged on friendly terms from the pamphlet war that ensued, Garrick undoubtedly believed that the Shylock role belonged uncontestedly and by priority to Macklin. When he entered into partnership with Lacy, he took over a company of the most skilled actors of the day, including Macklin as Shylock.

The Shylock that Macklin created was not likeable. On the contrary, the aspects of Shylock's personality that were stressed most by Macklin made the money-lender appear to be something of a monster. Macklin counted upon a shock-effect, and so fierce was this new Shylock that audiences were startled into taking him seriously for the first time. It was Macklin's underscoring of the Jew's malice and revengefulness that first established Shylock as a significant dramatic character. He was relentless, savage, ominous, venomous. So malignant was this Shylock that the spectators, un-

---

[2] 1748-49. Nicoll, *A History of Early Eighteenth Century Drama,* 1700-1750, p. 137. A complete listing of performances is included in C. B. Hogan, *Shakespeare in the Theatre,* 1701-1800.

[3] Ms. of one of Garrick's Drury Lane receipt books lists, on one occasion the profits of 2/10 for a *Merchant of Venice* evening, "For a young Gentlewoman in distress thro' ye Bankrupcy of her Guardian," Folger Shakespeare Library.

accustomed to such a display of passion on the stage, could not distinguish between the actor and his role and believed that in private life, Macklin was some sort of devil. As a matter of fact, Macklin had killed a fellow-actor in a quarrel over a wig in 1735. He had been tried for murder, and although he had been acquitted, playgoers probably recalled his violent disposition and associated it with the character he now portrayed.

The question of what it was that attracted Macklin to the Shakespearean play can hardly be resolved. Perhaps he was responding, more or less consciously, to a public demand for Shakespeare's plays in greater purity of text and plot.[4] It may be, too, that having achieved but slight distinction in minor plays, he was seeking a vehicle that would display his talents to better advantage, and found it in *The Merchant of Venice,* long overshadowed by the Granville version.

Possibly the best reason that Macklin had for undertaking to play Shylock was an awareness of his own personal suitability to the role. Portraits of him show dark, piercing eyes, an aquiline nose of considerable proportions, a short upper lip, a protruding lower lip and a massive jaw. He was above medium height, erect, athletic, robust without being corpulent. His face, even without make-up, suggests what Dickens later may have had in mind when he created Fagin.

The spirited Kitty Clive was cast as Portia, and doubtless this was a final concession to the farcical mood of the Granville era. She romped through the part in a flippant manner, mimicking Lord Mansfield, the famous lawyer, and introduced comical stage "business" in the trial scene in order to imitate his peculiarities which were then delighting London. Her burlesque of the young judge must have made Macklin's iron-visaged Shylock appear incongruous and ridiculous.

Shortly after Macklin's Shylock was introduced, Portia was given a song and it became the practice to list it in playbills: "Portia— With a Song." It was soon necessary for Lorenzo, Nerissa and Jessica, as well, to sing, and the number of musical selections con-

---

[4] Odell, *op. cit.,* p. 260.

tinued to increase.[5] In addition to the interpolated songs, novelties were introduced at the end of Acts III and IV which served to slacken the pace of the play. Evidently the eighteenth-century play-goer was in no greater hurry than his ancestors had been in Samuel Pepys' day. There was no attempt to sustain the play's unity by a discriminating choice of appropriate selections. Such extraneous pieces as *The Belle of the Village,* at the close of Act III and a dance entitled *The Arcadian Festival,*[6] following Act IV, literally served as divertissements. This concern with giving the public its money's worth in a variety program lasted until almost the close of the nineteenth century. Every sort of extravaganza, from acrobatic stunts to opera, shared the bill with *The Merchant of Venice.* Even with these distractions, the play continued to hold its own.

Although Macklin's genius brought about the innovation of a serious reading of Shylock's lines, a number of contemporary critics believed that he did not seem to have delved deeply enough into the character of the Jew and that he never succeeded in making the character come to life. His lasting popularity in the role, there-fore, remains something of a puzzle.

Macklin's stage career continued to be turbulent. By 1747, Garrick had begun his drive against the gentlemen-loungers who habitually sat on the stage or wandered behind the scenes to enhance the confusion that was usually associated with a performance. One of the receipt books for the Drury Lane during this period lists this matter-of-fact entry: "Feb. 22, 1748 . . . apple thrown at Macklin . . . I believe the main cause of this anger was their being refus'd admittance behind the scenes."[7] As late as 1773, *The Evening Post* reports an incident which indicates that the life of an actor in the eighteenth century was anything but smooth. Macklin was sched-

---

[5] Jessica's song

> Haste, Lorenzo, haste away
> To my longing arms repair,
> With impatience I shall die
> Come and ease thy Jessy's care.
> Let me then in wanton play
> Sigh and gaze my soul away.

was no great addition to the play, but it was undoubtedly profitable. It sold, apparently well, at one shilling a copy.

[6] Playbill for Covent Garden, November 15, 1781, Stead Collection.

[7] Garrick receipt books, Folger Shakespeare Library.

uled to appear as Shylock but: "The greatest part of the audience made an uncommon hissing, and called out, 'No play! No Macklin! Discharge him'!" When he came out, the uproar was so great he could not speak. After refusing to comply with the order to get down on his knees, he withdrew and the money was refunded to the spectators. The disturbance lasted two hours.[8]

It is said that Macklin had previously accused two rival actors of hissing him the preceding evening and that in retaliation his opponents staged this warm reception for his Shylock, but this explanation does not seem convincing. The audience in Macklin's day was far from sedate. So stormy, in fact, was the atmosphere in the theatre during this period that Macklin found it necessary to sue five of the ringleaders among the audience for conspiring to ruin his reputation. Although Macklin won the suit and was awarded damages, Lord Mansfield's decision accorded the playgoers the right to an instantaneous expression of their approbation or lack of it in the theatre.

Much has been written concerning Macklin's effort to dress his characters appropriately. Macklin's Shylock wore a loose black gown, long wide trousers and a skull-cap. His beard was short, red, wispy and pointed. This costume may represent a first attempt at historically accurate dress for Shylock, or it may be a further adaptation of the costume of Pantalone. William Cooke, Macklin's biographer, describes a dinner at which Pope, who was said to have seen Shylock on the third night of the first run, asked Macklin why he wore a *red* hat. The reply was that Macklin had read that Jews in Italy, particularly in Venice, wore hats of that color.

> "And pray, Mr. Macklin, do players in general take such pains?"
> "I do not know, Sir, that they do; but I had staked my reputation on the character, I was determined to spare no trouble in getting at the best information."
> "It was very laudable," said Pope.[9]

This little scene may never have taken place, but Pope's admiration of Macklin's performance has crystallized into a tradition which

---

[8] November 17, 1773.

[9] William Cooke, *Memoirs of Charles Macklin, Comedian,* London, 1806, p. 94 f.

has been handed on for endless quotation in the doggerel couplet invariably attributed to Pope:

> This is the Jew
> That Shakespeare drew.

During the long years that Macklin played the role of Shylock he must have found it necessary to modify his costume several times, and a number of changes are shown in later engravings, in which we find him in pantaloons and a Quaker collar that were much like the costumes worn by the Christians in the play. The pointed underchin beard, the skull-cap and the conspicuous hook nose remained as his "Jewish" markings.[10] His acting style in this part was evidently considered an authentic reproduction of Jewish manners and it was thought that much research had gone into it.

> When a comedian, celebrated for his excellence in the part of Shylock, first undertook that character, he made daily visits to the centre of business, the 'Change and the adjacent Coffee-houses, that by a frequent intercourse and conversation with the "unforeskinned race" he might habituate himself to their air and deportment. . . .[11]

William Cooke records what purports to be Macklin's description of his first performance of *The Merchant of Venice*:

> The opening Scenes, being rather tame and level, I could not expect much applause; but I found myself well listened to, — I could hear distinctly, in the pit, the words, 'very well — very well, indeed! — This man seems to know what he is about', &c. These encomiums warmed me, but did not overset me — I knew where I should have the pull, which was in the Third Act, and reserved myself accordingly. At this period, I threw out all my fire; and, as the contrasted passions of joy for the Merchant's losses, and grief for the elopement of Jessica, opens a fine field for an actor's powers, I had the good fortune to please beyond my warmest expectations. The whole house was in an uproar of applause — and I was obliged to pause between the speeches, to give it vent, so as to be heard. . . . The trial Scene wound up the fulness of my reputation: here I was well listened to; and here I made such a silent, yet forcible, impression on my audience, that I retired from this great attempt most perfectly satisfied. . . .[12]

---

[10] William Shakespeare, *The Merchant of Venice*, London, 1775.

[11] *Connoisseur*, January 31, 1754. William Cooke's memoirs of Macklin make no reference to such research.

[12] Cooke, *op. cit.*, p. 93.

Something of the pathetic quality of Shylock's plight may have come through in Macklin's interpretation. Davies says that it made some tender impressions on the spectators.[13] Macklin's fierceness, contrasting as it did with the sentimentalization of Shylock by later actors, would make it appear that these impressions were aroused by the character and not by the characterization. An account that probably has Macklin in mind describes Shylock, without Davies' reservation, as an abhorrent person:

> The wretched state to which Shylock . . . is reduced, is so agreeable a sacrifice of justice, that it conveys inexpressable satisfaction to every feeling mind. . . . [He is] . . . a most disgraceful picture of human nature; he is drawn, what we think man never was, all shade, not a gleam of light; subtle, selfish, fawning, irrascible and tyrranic. . . .[14]

The revival of the school of natural acting is usually credited to Garrick, although Macklin had done some important pioneering in this regard. Many years earlier he had been discharged from Lincoln's Inn Fields for speaking "too familiarly on the stage."[15] It is possible that some such mode of delivery helped him to fascinate and convince his audience with an unlovable Shylock. We have little direct evidence, but it is usually agreed that acting style before this time was highly artificial and elaborately stylized. Lines were spoken in oratorical fashion and were accompanied by equally unrealistic gesture. It was part of stage convention to employ "an elevated tone of voice, a mechanical depression of its tones, and a formal measured step in traversing the stage."[16] A contemporary writer described James Quin, a leading actor of this period as having

> . . . very little variation of cadence; and in a deep, full tone, accompanied by a sawing kind of action, which had more of the senate than of the stage in it, he rolled out his heroics with an air of dignified indifference, that seemed to disdain the plaudits that were bestowed upon him.[17]

---

[13] Thomas Davies, *Memoirs of the Life of David Garrick,* London, 1780, vol. I, p. 74.

[14] Francis Gentleman, *Dramatic Censor,* London, 1770, vol. I, pp. 278-291.

[15] Percy Fitzgerald, *The Life of David Garrick,* London, 1868, vol. I, p. 140.

[16] Cooke, *op. cit.,* p. 98.

[17] Richard Cumberland, *Memoirs,* London, 1806, p. 59.

Garrick's deportment on the stage was something else again:

> . . . alive in every muscle and in every feature. . . . What
> a transition! It seemed as if a whole century had been
> swept over in . . . a single scene; old things were done
> away, and a new order at once brought forward, bright
> and luminous, and clearly destined to dispel the barbarisms
> and bigotry of a tasteless age, too long attached to the
> prejudices of custom, and superstitiously devoted to the
> illusions of imposing declamation.[18]

While these and other bits of evidence may not be conclusive as
to the revolution brought about by Garrick, they indicate clearly
enough that something significant happened to the style of acting
in this period.

An account of Garrick's unusual histrionic quality furnishes us,
by inference, with some impressions of the declamatory style of his
contemporaries:

> . . . his voice was clear and piercing, perfectly clear and
> harmonious, without monotony, drawling or affectation; it
> was neither whining, bellowing, nor grumbling, but per-
> fectly easy in its transitions, natural in its cadence, and
> beautiful in its elocution. He is not less happy in his mien
> and gait, in which he is neither strutting nor mincing,
> neither stiff nor slouching. When three or four are on the
> stage with him, he is attentive to whatever is spoken, and
> never drops his character when he has finished a speech,
> by either looking contemptuously on an inferior performer,
> unnecessary spitting, or suffering his eyes to wander
> through the whole circle of spectators. His action is never
> superfluous, awkward or too frequently repeated, but grace-
> ful, decent, and becoming. . . .[19]

The battle that Garrick waged against the criticism of many actors
who feared that the use of a natural gait and of conversational
tones on the stage would impair the dignity of their profession
was obviously successful.

Three years after Macklin first appeared as Shylock, he established a school of acting at the Haymarket. The venture proved
to be unsuccessful, but it was there that he experimented with the
style of acting that he advocated. He would teach his pupils to
deliver a passage as they would in every-day life, preserving the

---

[18] *Ibid.*, p. 60.

[19] Cooke, *op. cit.*, p. 99.

same cadence, with amplification, for stage presentation. Eventually the methods of instruction that he advocated found their way into handbooks for student actors. In *Practical Illustrations of Rhetorical Gesture and Action*[20] we find the first careful analysis of Shylock's emotions, that may well represent Macklin's idea of characterization:

> Shylock experiences the most bitter anguish whilst recalling to his mind the previous jewels he has lost by the flight of his daughter: he evinces the most lively joy, whilst learning the catastrophe of Anthonio [sic], his rival in commerce, on whom he feels he can revenge himself at his pleasure. Accordingly, as his friend Tubal directs the attention of Shylock to the one or the other of these events, these two opposite sentiments alternately succeed in the soul of the Jew: grief seems to take the place of joy, and joy to assume that of grief, without any intermediate sentiment. I use the word *seems*, since grief, in succeeding to joy, no longer manifests itself with the same violence as in its original; and so joy, likewise, in its sudden triumph over grief, cannot, in its first instant, efface the wrinkles from the forehead, and restore it to all its natural serenity. With a feeble light, it smiles, as we may say, through a cloud, still leaving something of pain and chagrin in the first mien, and probably in the first tone of Shylock's voice; but the essential circumstance to be observed here is, that in joy there is found an *accessory* sentiment, which serves for its point of union with grief: I mean that joy arising from the misery of another person; consequently the joy of hatred, (of choler moderated) so closely approaches grief. The two alternate sentiments are not then simple, though they appear to be so.

Of the quality of Macklin's own speech, however, little is actually known. If the following passage from Churchill is any indication of Macklin's success as a teacher, his students would have done well not to heed their master:

> M–kl–n, who largely deals in half form'd sounds,
> Who wantonly transgresses Nature's bounds,
> Whose Acting's hard, affected, and constrained,
> Whose features, as each other they disdained,
> At variance set, inflexible and coarse,
> Ne'er know the workings of united force,
> Ne'er kindly soften to each other's aid,
> Nor shew the mingled pow'rs of light and shade,

---

[20] M. Engel, Adapted to the English Drama by Henry Siddons, London, 1807, pp. 356-67.

No longer for a thankless stage concern'd,
To worthier thoughts his mighty Genius turned,
Harangu'd, gave Lectures, made each single elf
Almost as good a speaker as himself;
Whilst the whole town mad with mistaken zeal,
An awkward rage of Elocution feel;
Dull Cits and grave Divines his praise proclaim
And join with Sheridan's their Macklin name.[21]

Frances Gentleman did not doubt that Macklin looked the part better than any other Shylock actor. He describes the range of emotion that Macklin demonstrated as the play progressed:

> . . . in the level scenes his voice is most happily suited to the sententious gloominess of expression the author intended; which, with a sullen solemnity of deportment, marks the character strongly; in his malevolence there is a forcible and terrifying ferocity; in the Third Act scene, where alternate passions reign, he breaks the tones of utterance and varies his countenance admirably; in the dumb action of the Trial Scene, he is amazingly descriptive.[22]

Lichtenberg, the German critic, saw Macklin play the part late in life. His observations on the subject are the best we have:

> Picture to yourself a somewhat portly man, with a yellowish coarse face, a nose by no means deficient in length, breadth or thickness, and a mouth, in the cutting of which Nature's knife seems to have slipped as far as the ear, on one side at least, as it appeared to me. . . . The first words he speaks on coming on the stage are slow and full of import. 'Three thousand ducats.' The two th's and the two s's, especially the last after the t, Macklin mouths with such unction, that one would think he were at once testing the ducats and all that could be purchased with them. This at starting at once accredits him with the audience in a way which nothing afterwards can damage. Three such words, so spoken in the situation, mark the whole character. In the scene where, for the first time he misses his daughter, he appears without his hat, with his hair standing on end, in some places at least a finger's length above the crown, as if the wind from the gallows had blown it up. Both hands are firmly clenched and all his movements are abrupt and conclusive. To see such emotion in a grasp-

---

[21] Charles Churchill, *The Rosciad*, London, 1763.

[22] Gentleman, *op. cit.*, vol. I, p. 291.

ing, fraudulent character, generally cool and self-possessed, is fearful . . .[23]

The effect was not intended to recommend Shylock to our sympathy. The writer concludes: "It is not to be denied that the sight of this Jew suffices to awaken at once in the best regulated mind, all the prejudices of childhood against this people."

Boaden was another who recalled the latter-day Shylock of Macklin:

> His acting was essentially manly,—there was nothing of trick about it. His delivery was more level than modern speaking, but certainly more weighty, direct, and emphatic. His features were rigid, his eye cold and colourless; yet the earnestness of his manner, and the sterling sense of his address, produced an effect in Shylock that has remained to the present hour unrivalled. Macklin, for instance, in the Trial Scene, 'stood like a TOWER,' as Milton has it. He was 'not bound to *please*' anybody by his pleading; he claimed a right grounded upon LAW, and thought himself as firm as the Rialto. To this remark it may be said, 'You are here describing Shylock.' True; I am describing Macklin.[24]

John Bernard is not nearly so respectful. He evidently regrets the passing of the musical style which the new school of acting had superseded. He remembers Macklin as "broad-breasted, shaggy-browed, hooked-nosed . . . as rough and husky as a cocoanut, with a barking or grunting delivery more peculiar than pleasing, which to musical ears made him something like a bore. . . ."[25]

There are, however, few disparaging notes in the chorus of praise for Macklin's performance. Doran recalls the reaction of the audience to the trial scene:

> The actor was not loud, nor grotesque; but Shylock was natural, calmly confident, and so terribly malignant, that when he whetted his knife . . . a shudder went round the house and the profound silence following told me that he held his audience by the heart-strings, and that his hearers

---

[23] George Christoph Lichtenberg, *Vermischte Schriften*, Goettingen, 1867, vol. III, p. 266.

[24] James Boaden, *Memoirs of the Life of John Philip Kemble*, London, 1825, vol. I, p. 440.

[25] John Bernard, *Retrospections of the Stage*, London, 1830, vol. II, p. 119.

must have already acknowledged the truth of his interpretation of Shakespeare's Jew. . . .[26]

Before long, Macklin's Shylock became the standard by which
to measure the interpretations of other actors in the role. The author
of the *Dramatic Censor* found Sheridan's treatment of Act I as
admirable as Macklin's, but inferior in the third and fourth acts.
King was not as cruel of feature or voice as Macklin and therefore,
not as good. Yates' conception was "insipid" and "disgraceful"
because he did not conceive Shakespeare's (or was it Macklin's?)
meaning. His manner must have differed considerably from that
of the master; it was described as "a quaint snip-snap mode of
expression."[27]

We have some notion of the disturbing quality of Macklin's
performance when we read how George II, on one occasion, was
so moved by the actions of this Shylock, that he could not sleep
the night he witnessed it.[28] *The Morning Post and Daily Advertiser*
reported of another performance, that when Shylock whetted his
knife, ". . . Mr. Macklin was so highly characteristic in the part,
that a young man who was in the pit fainted away."[29]

The half-century during which Macklin held the stage as Shylock
saw a great many changes in the theatre, but not much progress.
The eighteenth century was not productive of great English drama.
Farces were in their heyday, and what they lacked in quality was
more than compensated in quantity. Most of these farces served
as after-pieces, and shared the bill with the major presentation of
the evening. The age of the double-feature had begun!

Among the most popular farces of Macklin's era was *Love à la
Mode*, a product of Macklin's own pen, and the actor soon became
as well known for his creation of the haughty and miserly Sir
Archy MacSarcasm as he was for his Shylock. Another character
in Macklin's comedy was Beau Mordecai, an unfeeling, wealthy
Italian Jew, who is described in the play as a reptile. One writer
pictures

---

[26] John Doran, *"Their Majesties' Servants,"* New York, 1865, vol. II, p. 187.

[27] Gentleman, *op. cit.*, vol. I, p. 293.

[28] Bernard, *Retrospections of the Stage*, vol. II, p. 121f.

[29] November 9, 1781. Cited by Arthur Colby Sprague, *Shakespeare and the
Actors*, Cambridge, 1945, p. 27.

. . . the little Israelite's affectation of jauntiness or . . . the ignorant vanity which induces him to think everybody else is an object of ridicule, while he himself is the perpetual butt of the company.[30]

Macklin occasionally undertook both the roles of Sir Archy and Beau Mordecai in a single performance. Obviously, in Beau Mordecai, Macklin provided himself with the opportunity to display a comic counterpart of his Shylock. The program that was in greatest demand was the one that included *The Merchant of Venice* and *Love à la Mode*.

Following in the spirit of the tradition that was established by Granville's *The Jew of Venice* was a host of plays that depicted the Jew unfavorably, in the second half of the eighteenth century. The stage-Jew was irredeemably evil and miserly until after the Restoration. He then evolved into a less obnoxious type; but he was still caricatured and ridiculed. He had been a villain; he now became funny. It was this characterization that stubbornly persisted throughout the eighteenth century. The plays themselves, were insignificant; their characters wooden and incredible, but they held the interest of the public.

For the Jews who were living in England in the 1750's the acquisition of politically secured rights was a slow process. There were, at this time, 20,000 poverty-stricken Jews crowded into London's ghetto. Hordes of them had fled Germany and Poland following the Thirty Years' War. While England became a haven of refuge, it did not provide the civil security that the newly-arrived Jews sought there, although a handful of their co-religionists had already been granted political status in England. One Jew, Solomon de Medina, who had been financially useful to the Duke of Marlborough, had been knighted earlier in the century. But the few privileged families found their legal restrictions irksome; their descendants were not permitted to inherit their land and a number of them became converted to Christianity. These were the exceptions. The greatest part of British Jewry adhered to Judaism and was eager to gain political recognition in its own right.

In 1753, a bill for the naturalization of Jews was passed by the House of Lords. This created a furor and while it was eventually

---

[30] John Hunt, *Critical Essays of the Performers of the London Theatres*, London, 1807, p. 95.

passed by the Commons, public opposition to the bill was very great. Women were quick to take up the battle. They flaunted ribbons that bore the legend—"No Jews—Christianity for Ever;" they wore crosses around their necks and as decorations on their dresses; they arranged their *pompons* with crucifixes. Jew-baiting became a vogue. So widespread was the anti-Jewish sentiment, particularly in the merchant class—which looked upon the trend as a threat to its economic security—that public feasts of protest were held, where nothing but pork was served.[31] The demonstration bore results. The naturalization bill was repealed six months after it was introduced.

During this period, many Jews eked out a livelihood as petty traffickers—dealers in all sorts of used merchandise. The "old-clothes man" was a familiar sight on the streets and he soon found himself mimicked in songs and in plays, distorted in supposedly humorous caricatures. Besant tells us that when the costly coats and finely-embroidered velvets and silks that were worn by the men, and the thick, quilted petticoats and "gowns of stuff" that were part of women's apparel, were not bequeathed upon the death of their wearers, they were sold to Jewish itinerant peddlers, to be got up again and resold "as good as new." The Jewish peddlers were usually newly-arrived immigrants who had acquired neither the speech nor the social habits of the British. They presented, unquestionably, a bizarre appearance, and with their packs on their backs and their long beards, invariably invited the attention of boys on the street who greeted them with stones and with abuse.[32] Little by little, however, these Jews began to command a measure of respect. One observer recorded:

> I then saw the Jews being chased, whistled at, beaten, their beards plucked and spat at in the public street, without any passerby or officer of the law coming to their aid. . . . Dogs were not treated so shabbily as some Jews were. One circumstance above all others brought the mistreatment of the Jews to an end. In the year 1787 the Jew, Daniel Mendoza, became a famous boxer. He opened a school where he taught the art of boxing as a science. This sport spread

---

[31] Sir Walter Besant, *London in the Eighteenth Century*, London, 1903, p. 180.

[32] *Ibid.*, p. 177f.

rapidly among young Jews. . . . It was no longer whole-
some to molest a Jew if he did not happen to be an old
man. . . .[33]

Abroad, the struggle began to reap results. In 1791, the Jews of
France, who had been deeply involved in the struggle for the Rights
of Man, finally attained citizenship. The feeling of permanence and
self-esteem that came to French Jews enhanced the status of Jews
in other countries, as well. In America, Jews seized their first opportunity to fight shoulder to shoulder with their Christian compatriots
in the American Revolution. In England, progress came more slowly.
On the social scene, there was sporadic emancipation; a number of
Jews were coming to exert some influence in commerce, science
and the arts, and gradually the efficacy of portraying a murderous
and cruel Jew in the theatre was lost. Theophile Cibber, Fielding,
and O'Keefe saw the stage-Jew, instead, as a profligate; Knipe, Macklin and Sheridan made him out to be a ridiculous fool; Foote pic-
tured him as a would-be social climber; Morton drew him as a
hard-hearted master; while the other dramatists found him merely
detestable.[34]

But whatever the characterization might be, it required an actor
who could utilize make-up, gestures and speech in a very special
sort of way. Baddeley, Wewitzer, Quick, Dowton and Fawcett were
actors who could use Jewish dialect, or what Landa calls "gibber-
ish",[35] with devasting perfection and were amply rewarded with the
laughter for which they played. The "foreign accent" that they employed was, actually, English, generously interspersed with German
mispronounciations.

Richard Cumberland's play, *The Jew,* presented at the close of
the eighteenth century, was the first to break with the tradition
that employed a stock Jew for comic relief, and gave him some
humanitarian aspects. Its protagonist, Sheva, outwardly appears to
possess all of the customary traits of the usurer. In reality, he is a
saint. Sheva, however, is so overdrawn that he is dramatically un-
convincing; nevertheless, the play was successfully presented for the

---

[33] Francis Place, from an unpublished ms. in the British Museum Library,
cited by Fritz Heymann, *Der Chevalier von Geldern* in Nathan Ausubel,
A Treasury of Jewish Folklore, New York, 1948, p. 250.

[34] Edward D. Coleman, *The Jew in English Drama,* New York, 1943, p. xi.

[35] M. J. Landa, *The Jew in Drama,* London, 1926, p. 119ff.

first time in 1794 and it started a vogue for sentimental plays with long-suffering, whining and well-intentioned Jewish characters who were always vindicated in the end. This trend lasted as late as the twentieth century, when John Galsworthy's *Loyalties* made a new departure in an attempt to present the Jew as an integral part of society. In the case of *The Merchant of Venice,* it was not until 1879 when Henry Irving successfully demonstrated that Shylock could be played, not as a sinner, but as a man sinned against, that the stage-Jew finally attained dignity.

Cumberland wrote of Jewish personality, as it was presented on the stage in his day:

> . . . [it] is a mass of selfish corruption, and in fact, the Israelitish tribe has been so driven by the prejudices of society into a perpetual watchfulness after its immediate interest, that a Jewish mind is very often a mere camera obscura in which every surrounding object is represented in all its life, motion, and point of view, while the passing picture is completely hidden from outward observation and the room itself too confined to admit much sociality: in short, a Jew must become rich in order not to become utterly contemptible. But this is evidently not the fault of the Jew, *quatenus* Jew, as a logician would say, or merely because he is a Jew; there are at this moment men infinitely attached to the Jewish religion and customs, who have the art of getting rich and yet of preserving that liberality, which the weaker Israelite is afraid even to profess from a fear of the incredulity of his persecution; his enemies, he thinks, could exclaim with additional alarm against his miserly designs, were he to pretend generosity.[36]

During the long years in which these changes became manifest, interest in Macklin's Shylock continued unabated. Macklin played the role nearly fifty years. We read, how, at Covent Garden

> The house was uncommonly crowded and brilliant, and his reception very great. This wonderful old man, like Anteus, seems to acquire fresh vigour. . . .[37]

Two years later, the press notes that at the same theatre:

> . . . a crowded audience was collected . . . by what may be truly termed a phenomenon, a man in the ninetieth year

---

[36] Cumberland, *op. cit.,* p. 514, footnote in essay on Dowton's acting.

[37] October 14, 1786 notice of Covent Garden performance. No additional information. Stead Collection.

of his age, sustaining a character that requires the strongest exertions of faculties in their meridian blaze, and not merely sustaining them, but embodying them with such a force that would make the most inanimate spectator "live o'er the scene." A few trivial lapses of memory excepted, his performance of the character betrayed no symptoms of declension to the observation even of the oldest. On his entrance all hands and voices united in expressing the warm pleasure which the sight of him, who had entertained their fathers, and still retained the powers vigorous as the stoutest of their sons. . . .[38]

Added to the arduous role was the inconclusion in the program of *Love à la Mode,* in which the veteran appeared as Sir Archy. But old age was beginning to leave its inevitable marks on him. The loss of his teeth made his nose and chin appear to be more prominent. James Quin, a rival actor, remarked on the "cordage", not lines, in Macklin's face. With any other role, this would have been disastrous, but it suited the harsh and stern-faced Shylock that Macklin depicted. He had grown deaf and was unable to hear the prompter. Now his memory failed him and at last the Nestor of the stage, as he was called, was compelled to withdraw from the theatre.

As we review the contributions of other stage personalities, we shall see how each of them eventually succumbed to the onrush of new actors, new techniques and new taste. Macklin was the exception. There had been no dearth of Shakespearean actors in Macklin's time. His portrayal of a despicable Shylock never changed to suit the spirit of the times. But what he did, he did with such expertness that he was able to withstand the innovations that surrounded him. Even while he was in his dotage, he retained the title of having no equal in the role of Shylock. What he lacked in versatility—and his earlier failures with Macbeth and Richard testify to his limited range—he more than made up in the consistent and vigorous characterization of an avaricious and unrelenting Shylock.

---

[38] October, 1788 notice of Covent Garden performance. No additional information. Stead Collection.

EDMUND KEAN as SHYLOCK
Hiram Stead Collection
of the New York Public Library

CHAPTER III

Edmund Kean and His Era

EDMUND Kean was responsible for a number of significant innovations in acting that were subsequently incorporated into stage convention. His influence was felt during the years, early in the nineteenth century, when he shone as the brightest star in the theatrical firmament. Kean was the first to break with the tradition that made of Shylock a preposterous fiend. Macklin had built his reputation almost entirely on a conception of a stormy and diabolical Shylock, and although the veteran had been dead for almost two decades, the memory of his portrayal was kept green by the rank and file of actors who continued to find in *The Merchant of Venice* a rewarding role.

It took courage and imagination to dress Shylock in a black wig and to remold him so that his character would conform to his new appearance. It required an interpretation that would infuse credibly human qualities into what had become a mythical figure. Kean succeeded in accomplishing this. An actor's performance stands or falls with the support it receives from an audience, and the encouragement that Kean sought when he first presented his version of Shylock in London in 1814 came in surprising measure.

There was little justification for the hopefulness with which an actor normally undertakes a new role, when Kean first appeared as Shylock at the Drury Lane. A number of contemporary accounts report how only one rehearsal had been scheduled, the morning of the performance. Kean's portrayal had left the manager not only doubtful but disapproving. The actor had been assured that his characterization would not do, and now he was relying on his public to support him—the scant public that had witnessed not a single happy venture at the Drury Lane during the entire season. Kean did not have the benefits of a carefully-analyzed production that would integrate his interpretation with that of the other members of the cast. When his fellow-actors heard that he intended to play Shylock in a new manner, they were not only unprepared to support him, but were entirely hostile to him and to his proposed innovations, whatever they might be. The chief credit for the support of Kean's extraordinary performance goes, therefore, to the handful of spectators who first witnessed it.

The mode of acting that Garrick had established half a century earlier was characterized by polish and smoothness. Its techniques were possibly a vast improvement over the bombastic methods of the early eighteenth century, but Garrick's acting style made little distinction between the forceful and quiet, and it conveyed but little depth of character. When Kean first began to be noticed in 1814, it was to a considerable extent, for his energetic and sober portrayal. What was called demonstrative and passionate in his acting would undoubtedly now be considered extravagant and frantic. Nevertheless, he developed a style of acting that was known as "romantic" and it found adherents in such later practitioners as Junius Brutus Booth and Edwin Forrest.

Kean was only twenty-seven when he appeared as Shylock in that historic performance of January 26, 1814. Virtually unknown, wretchedly poor after years of hardship and privation, he staked his future on what he was convinced was the only valid delineation of Shakespeare's Jew. He was far from being a novice; the role of Shylock was not new to him. At the age of eleven, he had been featured as Edmund Craig, "the infant prodigy", and had astounded his listeners with dramatic readings. In this youthful repertory he included a recital of the complete text of *The Merchant of Venice*. The year prior to his Drury Lane debut, he had toured the provinces with a company and played the traditional Shylock over an extended period. We get some inkling of the demands made upon actors during this period, when we find Kean, on one occasion, billed as a dancer in a new *pas de deux* immediately following his Shylock appearance.[1] He had been brought up on a regimen of comedy,

---

[1] In a benefit performance for Kean in Totnes, August 6, 1813.

opera, farce and pantomime, in addition to tragedy—the one medium in which he demonstrated true skill. By 1814, he might well have grown stale in the Shylock role. Only a true artist could have conceived a fresh and original reworking of the character after so many years of routine acquaintance with the part.

The 1814 theatrical season was, as we have already noted, conspicuously unsuccessful, and performances at the Drury Lane were poorly attended. Kean found himself, during this period, in severe financial straits. He had never been free of the enveloping shadow of poverty. Hunger and poverty had hung about him as closely as the black cape he constantly wore to hide the meagerness of his person. The long, vain quest for approval and patronage, the memory of a miserable childhood, several years of which had been spent with his legs in straightening irons, the humiliation of being the bastard child of an erratic mother—these are not the ingredients of self-confidence—but they did much to give Kean insight and sympathy. He was willing to see in Shylock what no one but Shakespeare had seen—the tragedy of a man. For the rest, what was called a vigorous and brilliant performance was, in reality, a do-or-die struggle for existence. It was a matter of making a spectacular showing for once, or of ending a miserable career forever. His conviction must have been great indeed.

Kean, at this time, was small and thin, with an intense face and piercing eyes. An 1814 engraving shows his Shylock as a strong, handsome man with a short, trim beard, a cross on his left sleeve, and in his right hand, a butcher's knife.[2] Innumerable references have been made to Kean's bold use of a black wig for Shylock. This innovation may have been due simply to the fact that Kean's status at the Drury Lane was so precarious that he had to provide his own wig and costume.[3] It was no secret that the theatre had sustained 135 nights of continued losses and could not afford the expense of dressing the play adequately. We have no information that Kean owned a red wig at this time. He must have worn one during his earlier Shylock days in the provinces, but his frequent trips to the

---

[2] Stead Collection.

[3] "After dinner, Kean prepared for the awful evening. His stock of 'properties' was very scanty. He tied up his wig and collar . . . an old pair of black silk stockings, in a pocket handkerchief. . . ." B. W. Proctor, *The Life of Edmund Kean*, London, 1835, vol. II, p. 35.

pawnshop raise a question as to the extent of his wardrobe in 1814.

The outstanding actor of the day was John Philip Kemble. Kemble had adapted *The Merchant of Venice* for the modern stage in 1795 and had been the first to mount it with historical accuracy. A colored engraving that was issued five years before Kean's Drury Lane appearance, shows Kemble as Shylock in a skull cap, long robe, long black hair and a short, matching underchin beard.[4] An absence of comment on Kemble's use of a black beard leads us to suspect that this was an artist's conception and that he must have worn the kind of beard that was conventionally used for Shylock. The excitement over Kean's use of a black beard came too soon after this for Kemble's similar make-up to have passed unnoticed. Kemble's neatly-dressed Shylock had provoked some criticism; several reviewers did not consider him qualified by appearance to play the role.[5] In an attempt at realism, no doubt, he spoke Shylock's lines with a foreign accent and he encountered some disapproval because he "either growled in the same unvaried tone of utterance, or attempting to rise above himself like the winding of 10,000 Jacks."[6]

In the edition of the play that was revised by Kemble[7] "and now published as it is performed at the Theatre Royal, London . . . price one shilling and sold in the theatres" there are occasional Shylock speeches that are italicized for emphasis. Among these we find:

> *Hath a dog money? Is it possible*
> *A cur can lend three thousand ducats?*
>
> . . . .
> *Fair sir, you spit on me on Wednesday last;*
> *You spurn'd me such a day; another time*
> *You call'd me dog; and for these courtesies*
> *I'll lend you thus much monies?*

The absence, on the other hand, of any edifying markings in the "To bait fish withal" speech, the passionate "Why, there, there, there, there! A diamond gone . . ." or anywhere in the trial scene, leaves us uninformed as to Kemble's reading.

Kean seems to have borrowed little from Kemble. He had been

---

[4] Stead Collection.

[5] Timothy Plain, *Letters Respecting the Performances at the Theatre Royal,* Edinburgh, 1800, p. 55.

[6] *Ibid.*

[7] Printed for John Miller, 1814.

acclaimed for his ability to mimic Garrick's acting. As a boy he had appeared with the great Kemble and with Mrs. Siddons. If these associations inspired him at all, it was doubtless in a negative way. Kemble's technique had been characterized by its artificiality; Kean was to become noted for his sincerity. There was nothing lachrymose in Kean's style. He did not rely on declamatory powers. His great contribution to the theatrical development of *The Merchant of Venice* was in the degree to which he intellectualized his acting of Shylock.

When William Hazlitt recalled his first impressions of Kean's Shylock, not only did his description suggest the freshness and energy of the actor's portrayal, but it cast a backward glance at the delineation of earlier actors who had followed in the tradition of Macklin's Jew.

> When first we went to see Mr. Kean in Shylock, we expected to see what we had been used to see, a decrepit old man, bent with age and ugly with mental deformity, grinning with deadly malice, with the venom of his heart congealed in the expression of his countenance, sullen, morose, gloomy, inflexible, brooding over one idea, that of his hatred, and fixed on one unalterable purpose, that of his revenge. We were disappointed, because we had taken our idea from other actors, not from the play . . . a man of genius comes once in an age to clear away the rubbish, to make it fruitful and wholesome. . . . [8]

It was Kean's performance in 1817 that inspired Hazlitt[9] to take out of its original context the phrase "no less sinned against than sinning" and to apply it to Shylock.

Kean's Shylock did more than evoke sympathy; it startled his spectators. The first evidence of approval that Kean received came when his sparse audience of fifty burst into hearty applause following the line in his opening scene, "I will be assured I may."[10] The response must indeed have been balm to his soul. Dr. Drury reported that he could scarcely hold his breath when Kean first came on the stage as Shylock. "But directly you took your position," he later

---

[8] William Hazlitt, *Characters of Shakespeare's Plays*, New York, 1845, p. 178f.

[9] *Ibid.*, p. 174.

[10] William Shakespeare, *The Merchant of Venice*, edited by Henry Irving and Frank A. Marshall, New York, 1890, vol. III, footnote to Act I, Scene 3.

told the actor, "and leaned upon your cane, I saw that it was right."[11] Kean was, in fact, considered by many to be one of the best pantomime actors of his day.

In his interpretation of the Jacob and Laban speech, Kean played for time; Shylock had not yet hit on his scheme for vengeance. Toward the close of his speech to Antonio, he delivered the line, "you call'd me dog . . . ," with a voice of terrible passion, recovering himself just in time, and concluding with seemingly profound obsequiousness on "and for these courtesies I'll lend you thus much monies?". Here another enthusiastic outburst from the audience further dispelled his doubts as to the effectiveness of his interpretation.[12] He gained confidence, and with the acclaim he received for the fierce energy in the "Hath not a Jew eyes?" speech, he entered upon his kingship.

Hawkins describes the slightly deprecating manner in which Kean said "I am a Jew." Shylock's unmitigated miseries seemed to pass away in a moment when he reflected that the dignity of his race must not be hurt by his exciting commiseration in a Christian.[13] But it was in the scene with Tubal that Kean made his greatest impression. It is said that he raged like a lion. With the lines, "I would that my daughter were dead at my foot . . .", we are told that Kean

> . . . started back, as with a revulsion of paternal feeling from the horrible image his avarice had conjured up, and borrowing a negative from the next inquiry ('no news of them'?), gasped an agonising "No, no, no."[14]

The writer calls the spirit of this scene "the alternation of the two passions of anguished avarice and hopeful revenge."[15]

Many observers expressed the opinion that Kean's acting in the trial scene was anti-climactic compared with the overwhelming effectiveness of his scene with Tubal. A contemporary biographical study points to Kean's delineation here as a defect in characterization, describing it as a picture of a man stung into rage, rather than the

---

[11] Proctor, op. cit., vol. II, p. 37.

[12] Irving and Marshall, op. cit., vol. III, footnote to Act I, Scene 3.

[13] Frederick W. Hawkins, The Life of Edmund Kean, London, 1869, vol. I, p. 150.

[14] W. J. Fox, "W. C. Macready," The People's Journal, London, December 12, 1846.

[15] Ibid.

impersonation of the spirit of hatred.[16] But this is a comment of one who had come to accept the long-standardized personification of a vengeful Shylock as being the only valid one. On the other hand, Horace Howard Furness recalls his father's admiration of Kean in this scene; particularly for the

> . . . prolonged, grating, gutteral tone of utter contempt with which Kean's Shylock told Gratiano "Till thou canst rail this seal from off my bond. . . ."[17]

Gould illustrates Kean's powerful acting by the way in which his "Nay, take my life and all . . ." changed, by the pathos of his voice, the audience's hatred of Shylock, to one of pity.[18] We are told that Kean's entire appearance seemed to change with Shylock's last speeches. The pause in "I am—content," as if it almost choked him to bring out the last word; the partial bowing down of his seemingly inflexible will in "I pray you give me leave to go from hence, I am not well;" the horror of his countenance when he was told of his enforced conversion to Christianity; the combined scorn and pity with which he regarded the ribald Gratiano; his final exit, as he took with him the full measure of the audience's sympathy.[19]

The Theatrical Observer responded negatively to Kean's final exit as Shylock. It considered that Shylock should be

> . . . so completely overwhelmed . . . that he ought to repre-sent the mind in calm though bitter anguish. This style . . . loses all effect on the stage, by circumstances of the only power of expression to indicate this state of feeling, lying in the features . . . the perfect stillness of the frame, the clenched hands, and downcast eyes.[20]

In this criticism, there is revealed Kean's sympathetic, and even com-passionate treatment of Shylock. For the first time, the stage-Jew was taking on human form, and for the first time the audience was able to appreciate it.

During the early days of Kean's career, he was plagued by a fear of losing his voice. Several accounts describe the way in which he

---

[16] Proctor, *op. cit.,* vol. II, p. 46f.

[17] William Shakespeare, *The Merchant of Venice,* Horace Howard Furness, New Variorum edition, Philadelphia, 1895, p. 207.

[18] Thomas R. Gould, *The Tragedian,* New York, 1868, p. 74.

[19] Hawkins, *op. cit.,* vol. I, p. 152.

[20] February 15, 1825.

dashed from the stage to dressing room between the scenes on that famous opening night, eating oranges, in the hope that his voice would hold out. But what his voice lacked in durability was more than compensated in tonal quality. The use of conversational tones on the stage is a modern practice of the natural school of acting. In the early nineteenth century, actors employed an orotund method of delivery, sustaining their words in a singing manner. In this style, Kean was a virtuoso.

In a valuable study of Kean's voice, William Gardiner tells us:

> Musically speaking, he is the best orator, who, to his natural speaking voice, unites the upper and lower voices, that is, the *voce de testa* and the *voce de petto*. Mr. Kean possesses these qualifications in the highest degree. He has at his command the greatest number of effects, having a range of tones from F below the line to F above it . . . the natural key of his voice being that of B-flat. . . . His hard gutteral tone upon G is as piercing as the third string of a violoncello; whilst his mezzo and pianissimo expressions are as soft as from the voice of a woman. He has three distinct sets of tones; as if he occasionally played upon a flute, clarionet [sic], and bassoon, which he uses as the passion dictates . . . his notes are of the most touching and persuading kind, often springing from the harmonies of his natural voice, which he elicits with exquisite delicacy. . . . But the same voice, when moved with a ruder stroke, gave the yell and choked utterance of a savage.

His tones of furious passion are deep-seated in the chest, like those of the lion and tiger; and it is his mastery over these instinctive tones by which he so powerfully moved his audience. At times he vomits a torrent of words in a breath, yet avails himself of all the advantages of deliberation. His pauses give a grandeur to his performance, and speak more than words themselves.[21]

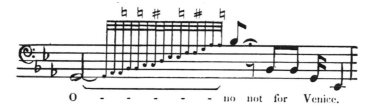

O - - - - - no not for Venice.

It has been said that Kean patterned his Shylock after the characterization of George Frederick Cooke, but there was apparent in Kean's interpretation so much less of the fiendish savagery than Cooke had exhibited, that we must doubt the statement. Only a decade before Kean appeared in London, the great Cooke and Mrs. Siddons were playing Shylock and Portia at Covent Garden. The introduction to a new edition of *The Merchant of Venice* called Cooke's Shylock

> . . . such a horrid picture of depraved nature, that we scruple not to pronounce him as original and high-finished a character as we can conceive, furnished with a most suitable peculiarity of style.[22]

The contrast between Cooke's style and Kemble's minute and studied manner had been observed by at least one critic who wrote:

> In soliloquies, especially, this superiority appears eminently conspicuous. He does not, after the example of the major part of the profession, cross and flounce about the stage; but conscious of the impropriety of *addressing a soliloquy to the audience,* delivers it as it ought to be delivered, as a kind of self-conference, in which a man may be said to be communing with his own soul.[23]

Leigh Hunt, in his *Autobiography,* recalled how unpleasant, like Cooke himself, was his Shylock. Cooke limited every character he undertook to its worst qualities, according to Hunt, and conveyed

[21] William Gardiner, *The Music of Nature,* Boston, 1837, p. 58f.

[22] William Shakespeare, *The Merchant of Venice,* Roach's edition, London, 1804.

[23] John Roach, *Authentic Memoirs of the Green Room,* London, 1801, p. 17.

no idealism, no affections and no feeling for verse in his interpretations.[24]

As Shylock, Cooke did not see himself as the center of interest
about whom the other characters of the play revolved. His acting
was not adorned with striking attitudes and studied gestures. The
uniformity and accuracy of his interpretation were in keeping with
what he believed to be the spirit of the text. Cooke did not play for
applause. His Shylock was consistently a shockingly depraved
demon. His inveterate hatred of Antonio was expressed by the manner in which he delivered "How like a fawning publican. . . ." One
account noted his bold sarcasm in the early scenes; the affected
levity and apparent carelessness with which he obtained the conditions of the bond; the subsequent triumph and anticipated revenge.[25]
The flight of his daughter found Cooke's Shylock in a state of agitation, disorder and misery; while his joy over Antonio's misfortunes
was portrayed by "the alternate passions of avarice and revenge."
He was exultant in the trial scene. He whetted his knife on the
floor, while he watched Antonio with savage determination.

> But it is not until the judge commands Antonio to bare his
> bosom to the knife of Shylock, that the whole force and
> comprehension of Cooke's genius bursts forth in its meri-
> dian splendor. Upon Portia's enumerating the rigid con-
> ditions upon which the forfeit was to be obtained, no
> language can do justice to the excellence of Cooke. His
> countenance in an instant lost its wonted glow of malicious
> satisfaction, and became horribly convulsed with disap-
> pointed rage. His manner of dropping the scales at the
> annihilation of his hopes, was strongly indicative of the
> writhing tortures of a despairing soul. When Antonio
> offers to remit half of his estate, on condition of leaving the
> other half to the use of Lorenzo, and of his immediately
> embracing the Christian religion . . . the groan of con-
> vulsive agony that seemed to burst from the very inner-
> most recesses of his soul, was electric in its effects.[26]

When Cooke died, in 1812, many felt that the role of Shylock
had expired with him. We have seen how young Kean excelled him
in the part two years later, with an interpretation that departed from
all former models.

[24] Leigh Hunt, *Autobiography*, New York, 1850, vol. I, p. 158.

[25] *Evening Post*, November 30, 1810.

[26] *Ibid.*

Theatrical annals tell of Kean's increasing popularity after his London debut. He had been eager to play Shylock largely because his puny figure made it an appropriate part in a necessarily limited repertory; the role became his chief glory as an actor. His originality became more perceptible as his Shylock matured. Thanks to him, the Drury Lane was now once more on its feet. Kean played Shylock fifteen times out of his seventy appearances that first season; this was considered a record for the part. He soon took on other roles; notably Richard III, Othello and Sir Edward Mortimer; but Shylock remained, basically, close to his original conception. He did not alter Shylock's costume extensively. A list of the costumes for an 1820 production describes Shylock's attire as consisting of a black gabardine with a crimson vest and a black hat.[27]

It was during this time that the name of William Charles Macready, already one to be reckoned with in the theatre, became associated with the role of Shylock. It was almost a decade after Kean's initial success with the part that Macready first experimented with it. In 1823, in a performance for his benefit at Covent Garden, he appeared in *The Merchant of Venice* with Charles Kemble, son of the eminent John Philip Kemble, who played Bassanio. Macready wrote candidly of that first performance:

> The audience, ever disposed to look with favor on my attempts, were most liberal in their applause, but I was not satisfied with the executions of my conceptions, which the study of after years very greatly improved.[28]

He was envious of Kean's popularity as Shylock and as late as 1850, long after the generation that recalled Kean's portrayal ceased to exist, Macready appeared in the role, both in England and America. It was never one of his favorites. His fine reputation as Hamlet and other Shakespearean characters served to carry him in *The Merchant of Venice* role, but he never seemed fully equipped for it and he was never content with his characterization. He wrote in his diary in 1841: "My reception was most enthusiastic. I acted Shylock very nervously—not to please myself . . ."[29]

[27] William Shakespeare, *The Merchant of Venice,* W. Oxberry edition, London, 1820.

[28] Sir Frederick Pollock, *Macready's Reminiscences,* New York, 1875, p. 202.

[29] William Barr Toynbee (edited by), *The Diaries of William Charles Macready,* London, 1912, vol. II, p. 151.

WILLIAM CHARLES MACREADY as SHYLOCK
From the author's collection

He did, however, please the critics and he was unanimously praised for the over-all excellence of his production. His effective settings, his judicious discarding of the musical solos and duets with which his contemporaries continued to hamper the action of the play, his reliance on "the text of Shakespeare," as announced in the advertisements, all combined to emphasize the drama and the poetry of the play. The public rewarded his efforts with such enthusiastic response that it became necessary to publish the statement for the Haymarket revival in 1839, and again in 1842, at the Drury Lane, that "In consequence of the overflow to all parts of the theatre, *The Merchant of Venice* will be repeated twice a week 'till further notice." During his last years, Charlotte Cushman shared the honors with him in her portrayal of Portia. His costume for Shylock was observed with approval. A daguerrotype shows his short, cropped beard, his long hair and the neat, rich clothing that gave the impression of a picturesque and dignified Jew.[30]

George Henry Lewes believed that Macready had few rivals on the stage in his ability to express tenderness, but he found him unsuited to extremely tragic roles.[31] Macready's restrained stateliness on the stage contrasted sharply with the declamatory force, the emotionalized mood and the frantic gestures that characterized Kean's acting in his earlier days. Kean conceived the character of Shylock as a persecuted martyr who, through the forces of circumstances, finally became an avenger. Macready thought of Shylock as a man who was composed of harshness.

A number of his fellow-actors considered Macready an embittered man and a nervous actor. One of them called him "a dreadful man to act with."[32] While he continued to play the part with earnestness, he was obviously out of his depth in interpreting Shylock as a complex personality. To simulate the proper pitch of excitement, in order to express convincingly Shylock's intense rage, he had to work himself artificially into a state of agitation before making his entrances and it was reported that he used to spend some minutes in

---

[30] Houghton Library, Harvard University.

[31] George Henry Lewes, *On Actors and the Art of Acting,* London, 1878, p. 42.

[32] Mrs. John Drew, quoted by Odell, *Annals of the New York Stage,* New York, vol. V, p. 4.

the wings, lashing himself into an imaginary state of fury by swearing under his breath and by violently shaking a ladder that was attached to a wall backstage.[33]

A prompt-book that may have belonged to Macready demonstrates his regard for Shakespeare's text. The jailer scene is included, as well as Act V,[34] at a time when a number of his contemporaries had already deleted the final scene. In the malice and cruelty of Macready's Shylock, no note of humanity was expressed in the lament over the loss of Leah's ring; there was only petulant regret for the disappearance of a valuable jewel. In his handling of the trial scene, one writer found "an instance of subtle blending of the chief motives of a part with its national features."[35] The Jew's traditional reverence for law and his belief in its inviolability were emphasized in Macready's reading of the lines: "If you deny me, fie upon your law!;" "Is that the law?"[36] This Shylock was neither extraordinary nor conventionally excellent, but it held the interest of the public that was always ready to respond to an actor of prestige.

Almost from the outset, lesser actors took to imitating Kean's Shylock. Several of them featured their presentations as *Shakespeare's Tragedy of the Merchant of Venice*. Meanwhile Kean continued patiently to build his reputation, largely on his Shylock, and the encomiums steadily mounted. George Henry Lewes, however, who saw Kean act in 1825, seven years before the actor quit the stage, called Kean's style tricky and flashy. He found his acting lacking in dignity, and stressed Kean's limitations and his inflexibility in the range of expression. Kean, he thought, was incapable of simulating laughter, gaiety or playfulness and he considered him to be an imperfect mime. But he was a master of tragedy. Tenderness, wrath, agony and sarcasm were at his command, according to Lewes, though he could not be calm or stately. "He was nothing, if not passionate."[37] It was impossible to watch Kean's Shylock

> . . . without being strongly shaken by the terror, and the pathos, and the passion of a stormy spirit uttering itself in

---

[33] Lewes, *op. cit.*, p. 44.

[34] Folger Shakespeare Library.

[35] Westland Marston, *Our Recent Actors*, Boston, 1888, p. 101.

[36] Prompt-book that probably belonged to Macready, Folger Shakespeare Library.

[37] Lewes, *op. cit.*, p. 9.

tones of irresistible power. The overpowering remonstrant sarcasm of his address to Antonio, and the sardonic mirth of his proposition about the 'merry bond' were fine preparations for the anguish and rage at the elopement of his daughter, and for the gloating anticipations of revenge on the Christians. Anything more impressive than the passionate recrimination and wild justice of argument in his 'Hath not a Jew eyes?' has never been seen on our stage.[38]

Colerbridge's often-quoted remark that Kean's acting was like "reading Shakespeare by flashes of lightning" and Douglas Jerrold's comparison of Kean's Shylock with a chapter of Genesis suggest the dramatic intensity that he must have conveyed. Much has been said of Kean's relentless insistence on the representation of a dogmatic Jew in the spirit of "an eye for an eye." It was this quality that led a number of writers to insist that Kean was, himself, a Jew, since no one but a Jew could infuse Shylock with this awesome and terrifying tone of Hebraic majesty.

Kean has often been called the first great "star," whatever this may mean, and he has been accused of having undertaken Shakespearean roles only for the purpose of exhibiting his own talents; his abbreviated versions of the scenes in which he did not appear are sometimes taken as evidence against his basic interest in Shakespeare. But when we compare Kean's treatment of the play with the liberties that were yet to be taken in the juggling of scenes, the omission of characters and the deletion of the entire fifth act, we must conclude that Kean handled *The Merchant of Venice* with reverence and was but moderately concerned with glorifying himself in a stellar role. In his production of the play, only those characters which appeared in Act V were present at the final curtain. Shylock did not take a bow.[39]

The role of Shylock was Kean's supreme contribution to the theatre. He did not always apply the same fiery energy to his other dramatic characters. His portrayal of Barabas in *The Jew of Malta* was inexplicably ineffective; his Abel Drugger was a failure. Kean could not play farce. Hazlitt hailed his naturalistic acting—the very quality for which he was disliked in Paris. A number of the younger literary critics were his admirers—Byron and Leigh Hunt; but his

---

[38] *Ibid.*, p. 11.

[39] Chart of disposition of characters, W. Oxberry edition.

popularity finally brought about his undoing. He grew restless. One triumphant tour in America encouraged a second and disastrous one. His shortcomings were becoming conspicuous. Kean had never known how to integrate his parts with his plays. As time went on, he disregarded more and more the principle of unity, and rarely achieved a complete and harmonious conception of character. As he gained acclaim, his acting became a series of uneven dramatizations, and his reputation as a virtuoso who was concerned for nothing but his own performance at last was justified.

The early part of Kean's first American tour, during the 1820-21 season, was eminently successful and *The Merchant of Venice* was a featured presentation.[40] The play was billed as *Shylock*. It had become a starring vehicle for Kean. Nevertheless, New York play-goers found his Shylock so stirring that on one occasion they afforded it the rare tribute of not applauding. He was said to be the most complete actor that had never appeared in the city.[41] On arriving in Boston, he met with no such approbation. Business was poor the first two nights of his engagement, and finding only twenty people in the house on the third night, he decided not to go on. But the public that had failed to attend his performances was not too indifferent to create an incident. Kean's failure to appear was considered a gross insult to the city of Boston, and other communities took up the matter and amplified it. The press became an effective ally. No amount of public apology availed the actor, and gaining neither support nor sympathy, he hastily fled for home. England, however, was no haven of refuge for him at this time. He had long been frowned upon for his tippling and other dissipations, and a notorious affair with the wife of Alderman Cox had been his chief reason for going to America. By 1825 on his return to the States, Boston had built up a convincing case against Kean, and its moral-

---

[40] It is interesting to note that it was *The Merchant of Venice* that was, according to Dunlap, "the first play performed in America by a regular company of comedians." (William Dunlap, *A History of the American Theatre*, New York, 1832, p. 8.) It was presented by the Hallams, with Malone as Shylock, at Williamsburg, then the capital of Virginia, on September 5, 1752. (Arthur Hobson Quinn cites evidence for September 15 as the correct date. *A History of the American Drama, From the Beginning to the Civil War*, New York, 1923, p. 10 ftnote.)

[41] *Post*, December 4, 1820.

istic attitude concerning the actor's personal life served to bar him
from appearing in that city at all.

The objections to Kean seem to have been of a piece with the
earlier dictum of Robert Treat Paine, Boston signer of the Declara-
tion of Independence, who had expressed his high opinion of the
social influence of the theatre.

> We are deeply impressed with the belief that the theatre
> is highly important to society as a great publick school in
> which all classes may assemble, to acquire mutual respect
> from examples of good breeding, to cultivate morality from
> the delineations of life.[42]

The editorial comments, in their reference to the actor's morality,
indicate some of the early nineteenth century outlook on what it
believed to be shocking social behavior. The occupational hazards
of the acting profession were considerable at this time.

When Kean finally appeared, after the boycott was lifted in
several cities, the press was noticeably cool. *The American* was
pleased to note that "not a single respectable female appeared in
the house." Whether related to this expression of public opinion
or not, there was now evident in Kean's acting a prim, almost
pedantic quality that was considered to be a vast improvement over
his former brash style. He was cited for maintaining a "chasteness
and propriety" that were foreign to his earlier acting.[43] *The Albion,*
too, noted Kean's newly acquired dignity and paid him the dubious
compliment of praising him for his departure from his habitual
hysterical laughter, his ranting tone and his use of stage tricks.[44]
Molloy, his biographer, concedes that his style was modified because
his spirit was broken and that his former fire now blazed only
intermittently. The world had tamed him.[45]

The concessions that Kean made to public taste reaped some
benefits for him. One year later, having recaptured a measure of
his early appeal in America, he was again appearing before full
houses. He had abandoned, for good, the old showy stunts of

---

[42] Quoted by Montrose J. Moses, *The American Dramatist,* Boston, 1925,
p. 80f.

[43] November 15, 1825.

[44] Cited by J. Fitzgerald Molloy, *The Life and Adventures of Edmund Kean,*
London, 1897, p. 351.

[45] *Ibid.,* p. 350.

starting suddenly and pausing unexpectedly. But along with these, he had lost much of his zest for acting and for living. He had become resentful, and his style reflected it. Fanny Kemble saw him play Shylock in 1827 and wrote that he "entirely divested Shylock of all poetry or elevation, but invested it with a concentrated ferocity that made one's blood curdle."[46]

The Shylock of Samuel Phelps and of Robert Campbell Maywood were greatly admired during Kean's last years, but it was in Edwin Forrest that he encountered his keenest rival. Forrest was a mere boy when he first played Shylock in 1826, but his youthful and energetic talent served to diminish Kean's glory. Forrest's tendency to overact and to emotionalize his characterizations were decried. He was, actually, a satellite of Kean's, but the intellectual maturity of his readings was already noticed and it won for him the praise that had once belonged to Kean alone. The vigor of his acting overshadowed the techniques of the older man. When Kean returned to England for the last time, he was disappointed and spent, old before his time and already forgotten by the world that had once hailed him as incomparable.

One successful attempt to convince an audience with an original reading came at the time when Kean's interpretation still continued to exercise influence on Shylock actors. In 1834, an obscure actor, H. G. Denvil, presented a vigorous and confident Shylock. His self-possessed manner, his elastic step and audacious sarcasm introduced a Shylock to which the public was unaccustomed, but which must have, unconsciously, impressed itself on the Victorian mind. Denvil's acting has never been singled out as exemplifying the best of its day, and evidences of its significance, in the Shylock role, at least, are to be found only in long-forgotten "Theatrical Intelligence" columns and in the praise that later actors received for interpretations that strongly resemble his invention. Macready, with whom he appeared briefly in other roles, noted grudgingly in his Diaries, "I apprehend that he has something in him beyond the common run."[47]

The Shylock of Denvil bullied Antonio with an easy air of indifference and superiority. He conveyed a genuinely gentle and

---

[46] Cited by Brander Matthews, Shakespearean Studies, reprint, New York, 1916, p. 17.

[47] Toynbee, The Diaries of William Charles Macready, vol. I, p. 187.

genial spirit in his leave-taking of Jessica; the repose in his demeanor only subtly suggesting his uneasy sense of impending calamity. But he was more energetic than passionate in the scene with Tubal, and in the conclusion of the "To bait fish withal" speech, he was so resolute in his "revenge," that he said the word, not once, but three times. "Noise was the climax," read one report.[48] It was not until the very end that his mood deepened and darkened. In the trial scene, he was the injured and insulted Jew who recollected Antonio's merciless taunts and all the savage persecution against his people. He strove to look contemptuously at Gratiano, but his spirit failed. He turned and attempted to raise his head, but could not. When he finally staggered out of the courtroom in desolate despair, it was felt that he had not only been vindicated for his excesses, but that he had pointed up the hypocrisies of his persecutors, and made the remainder of the play inconsequential and ineffective.

Obviously, this conception of Shylock was somewhat ahead of its time. *The Examiner,* in reviewing Denvil's performance, took him to task for his lofty conception of the Jew in the early parts of the play. It considered his characterization of a vital Shylock as being "absurdly incorrect," calling attention to Shakespeare's use of the phrase "old Shylock." Denvil bowed to these criticisms. *The Examiner* was pleased to note the way in which Denvil had moderated his reading in a subsequent performance.[49]

The England that had applauded Kean's Shylock in the first quarter of the nineteenth century, continued to show a lively, and for the first time, a friendly interest in the Jews. The repeated attempts on the part of the Jews to gain a foothold in the country in which their families had dwelt for generations, were beginning to be rewarded with some success. There were twenty thousand Jews in England at the opening of the century; many of them were on the humblest social level—the peddlers and hawkers on the streets, but a number of them had distinguished themselves. Yet all of them were aliens in England. In 1820, however, Jews were admitted to the Bar; in 1835, to the Shrievalty; in 1843, to other municipal offices. Finally, through the gradual repeal of many clauses in the Uniformity Act and the Laws of Recusancy, the

---

[48] *Examiner,* an unidentified clipping, Stead Collection.
[49] *Examiner,* unidentified clipping, Stead Collection.

Religious Opinions Relief Bill was passed in 1846. The Jews' minor disabilities were removed, their welfare formally looked to in specific provisions and their legal rights established. The following year, Baron Lionel de Rothschild was elected to Parliament. He was the first professing Jew to be accorded the honor, but it was not until eleven years later, when the oath of office finally was amended to relieve him of the scruple of repeating "upon the true faith of a Christian," that he took his seat.

Now nineteenth-century liberalism was in full bloom in England, but there was no such flowering in the shaded corners of the world. The Damascus Blood Libel in 1840, and the Mortara Affair in Italy in 1858, aroused sorrowful concern and brought additional Jews to England. Meanwhile, the current literary magazines were devoting generous space to subjects of Jewish interest. Active evangelical work was being done among Jews. In the theatre, plays with Jewish characters continued to be popular. In 1820, four different dramatizations of Scott's *Ivanhoe* appeared, prominently featuring the Isaac and Rebecca story. *The Jew and the Doctor* and *Sarah, thé Jewess* were stage favorites in the '40s.

If any additional reason beyond the sheer love of the theatre is necessary to explain public interest in the Shylock of Edmund Kean and that of his son, Charles, it may be found in the development of these trends. In Charles Kean's impersonation of Shylock there was something of the same vigorous quality that Edmund Kean had once displayed. The son retained much of his father's reading of an indignant, unsentimentalized Jew who rightfully fought to the end for his revenge. This was the conception that the early Victorians, who had been brought up on Macready's portrayal, knew and admired. They felt that Shylock had been wronged, but that despite his bitterness and anguish, he kept his dignity and grandeur, and the result was a Manfred-like character dear to the romantic soul.

Charles Kean, however, had few natural gifts. In addition to the unreliable voice and the insignificant figure that he inherited from his father, he was a poor actor. His face lacked expressiveness and there was insufficient impulse in his acting. In view of his shortcomings, it is understandable that he should have turned to an intellectualized style of acting and that he should have become a pioneer in stagecraft. He was reasonably successful.

In 1848, he was honored by an invitation to present *The Merchant of Venice* before Queen Victoria at Windsor Castle. His wife, the former Ellen Tree, who had played Portia so frequently during her stage career, retained that role on this occasion. It must have been in deference to the dignity of the event that the usual farce, such as *A Kiss in the Dark* or *My Wife's Mother,* favorites in the younger Kean's *Merchant of Venice* bill, was not included by Her Majesty's servants in the royal entertainment.

Charles Kean wrote in his preface to his acting edition of *The Merchant of Venice:*

> The costumes and customs are represented as existing about the year 1600, when Shakespeare wrote the play. The dresses are chiefly selected from a work by Caesar Vecellio, entitled *Dagli Habiti Antichi e Moderni di Venetia, 1590:* as well as from other sources found in the British Museum. . . .[50]

Playgoers had already evinced unusual interest in the settings for the play in a Drury Lane presentation in 1833. This apparently had more merit as a travelogue than as a dramatic performance; it featured Stanfield's "celebrated views of Venice." Kean evidently adapted this earlier production to his purposes. But with this emphasis on staging, Kean reduced Shakespeare's play to not much more than a magnificent show, and the scene-mechanic became as important to him as the actor, who, overwhelmed by the elaborate scenery and costuming, functioned as a mere assistant in the display. Careful stage delivery was no longer regarded as essential to the actor and many critics have accused Charles Kean of fostering the poor style of delivery that came to be characteristic of later acting.

Charles Kean was essentially a stage technician and it was by dint of sheer effort in that direction that he made his mark. He was the first of the modern actors to concern himself with the mechanics of staging. The elaborate details of his stage sets, the technical devices, the decorative effects and the vast numbers of supernumeraries he employed, tended somewhat to obscure the play. It was Kean's custom to advertise in the cities in which he was about to appear for as many as one hundred "extras." But if Kean overemphasized the staging of his plays, his efforts were, at

---

[50] London, 1858.

least, away from the utter indifference that his predecessors mani-
fested in this regard. It was his aim to achieve integrated and well-
balanced productions and his revivals in the 1850's reached a peak
in the display of pageantry.

Through Charles Kean's presentation of *The Merchant of Venice,*
there passed throngs of nobles, citizens, inquisitors, traders, foreign-
ers, water-carriers and flower girls. During one period, he employed
a little girl whose function it was to carry a basket of doves. The
little girl was to become the greatest Portia of all time. She was
Ellen Terry. Audiences were impressed, too, by the bridge that
arched the canal in the street scene, over which Jessica and the
others could actually cross and under which gondolas passed. It
was most spectacular.

Charles Kean loved to manage large groups of people. Everything
was complicated on his stage. He gave Antonio a servant in addition
to a clerk and minstrels (although he omitted Morocco and
Arragon). There were in the trial scene no fewer than twenty-six
judges and forty senators as well as the necessary heralds and
unnecessary servants, captains and esquires.[51] When the last of the
hundred supernumeraries was placed in the courtroom, the stage
was definitely full. If the principal characters could be made out
at all, their actions must have been lost against such a welter of
color and movement.

Although Charles Kean's acting left no lasting impression, his
lavish staging was not soon forgotten. This overemphasis on the
mechanics of the production was not without its effect on the
development of *The Merchant of Venice* in the theatre, for later
presentations were to show evidences of the results of the younger
Kean's striving for historical authenticity in the play.

---

[51] Charles Kean's prompt-book. Folger Shakespeare Library.

EDWIN BOOTH as SHYLOCK
Walter Hampden Memorial Library
at The Players, New York

CHAPTER IV

Edwin Booth

WHEN Edwin Booth first announced that he would play
Shylock, it was expected that the representation of the
son would resemble that of Junius Brutus Booth as closely
as Charles Kean had reflected Edmund Kean's delineation of the
role. The Shylock of Junius Brutus Booth had been archetypical.
The elder Booth had evinced an understanding and sympathy for
Jews in general. He had more than a passing acquaintance with
Jewish ways. He was said to have attended a synagogue with some
regularity and to have been able to participate in the service in
Hebrew. His study of the Talmud and his strict adherence to some
of its dicta have also been adduced. It seems highly questionable
that Booth knew much Hebrew, if any. He was praised for de-
livering Shylock's speeches in Hebrew[1] at a time in his career when
no Hebrew translation of the play existed and we are led to
conclude that he played the part in dialect, with a Yiddish accent—
a Shylock convention that continued to be persistently popular.

During the early decades of the nineteenth century, dozens of
plays were written for the express purpose of presenting the stage-
Jew.[2] A command of "broken English" and the sing-song inflection
that was supposed to convey the speech patterns of Jews in England
at this time, was considered an indispensable part of the equipment
of the comic actor. An exaggerated use of hand gestures and shrugs
was supposed to suggest further the ridicule-provoking peculiarities
of a people who were now furnishing a new stock-character. The
majority of the Jews in England at this time were neither eco-
nomically nor socially assimilated into British life. Many had found

---

[1] At Covent Garden, September 17, 1818.

[2] For footnote 2 see p. 64.

roots in the course of centuries, but their newly-arrived co-religionists from other countries exhibited foreign mannerisms that were uncomfortably conspicuous to the more secure citizenry—Jew and non Jew alike.

For all of his admiration of Jewish practices, Junius Brutus Booth is said to have found the religious forms of other faiths equally appealing. He professed a similar appreciation for the Koran and for the teachings of Catholicism. It is reasonable, therefore, to suspect that his interest in Jewish ceremonies and customs was somewhat more superficial than his biographers believe. That his Jewish interests provided a background for his understanding of Shylock cannot be denied. His portrayal stressed the two factors that motivated Shylock's hatred of Antonio. He hated him, first, because he was a Christian and second, because the merchant had hindered his usurious practices. Thomas R. Gould points up the differences between Booth's Shylock and the version that was then generally popular on the stage:

> The superficial features of the Jew's character are patent to everyone — his greed, his miserliness, his implacable revengefulness; — but in the refined handling of this great artist, these traits were made the mere outworks behind which was seated a grand reserved force. . . . The Jew . . . wrapped up in himself the dignity of the patriarchs of his people. . . . Booth . . . knew how to assume the Hebraic standpoint . . . the conception of a people selected as the guardian and minister of . . . law. . . . Booth embodied all this gloomy grandeur of position, this merciless absolute-

---

[2] Thomas Dibdin's *The School for Prejudice*, presented at Covent Garden, 1801, renamed *The Lawyer, The Jew and The Yorkshireman* in an 1825 revival, depicts an "honest" Jew. This was followed by Dibdin's *Family Quarrels*, at Covent Garden, 1802, with a character in Jewish disguise who sang a song that offended the Jews in the audience and caused a disturbance. Thomas Holcroft's *Hear Both Sides*, produced at the Drury Lane, 1803, featured a bailiff who spoke in Yiddish dialect and was cited by Charles Lamb in *On the Custom of Hissing in the Theatres*. James Kenny's *Ella Rosenberg*, adapted from the French, Drury Lane, 1807, was a two-act melodrama with the villain masquerading as a Jew. John Till Allingham's *Transformation; or Love and Law*, Lyceum, 1810, was a musical farce featuring a Jew and another character in Jewish disguise. Both spoke "broken English." W. T. Montcrieff's three-act musical comedy, *Rochester; or King Charles Second's Merry Days*, at the Olympic, 1818, finds two characters in Jewish "old-clo'" disguises, pretending to speak Hebrew. Henry M. Milner's *The Jew of Lubeck*, Drury Lane, 1819, has its protagonist, denounced as a traitor, disguising himself as a Jew. The list can be extended.

ness of will. . . . He made it the *representative Hebrew:* the type of a race as old as the world. He drew the character in lines of simple grandeur, and filled it with fiery energy. In his hands it was marked by pride of intellect; by intense pride of race; by a reserved force, as if there centered in him the might of a people whom neither time nor scorn, nor political oppression could subdue. . . .[3]

Later critics held with the opinion that the elder Booth gave to the role all the energy and abandon it required, but his techniques were summed up by Walt Whitman as being inflated, stagey and antiquated.[4]

With the son, it was another matter. Edwin Booth seems in general to have stepped into his father's shoes with ease, but his attempt at the role of Shylock came hesitatingly. His first appearance as the Jew was in Australia. The seventy-two day journey from San Francisco must have afforded him ample time to analyze the part, for he had a rewarding engagement there. Three years later, he made his New York debut in the theatre that Dion Boucicault was later to call the Winter Garden, and he included Shylock in his repertory.

In 1861, at the request of the management at the Haymarket, he began his first London engagement with *The Merchant of Venice*. British theatre-goers were accustomed to respond somewhat negatively to visiting American actors in "British" roles, and they made no exception in this case. The British were evidently devoted to the Shylock of the Keans, and were not willing to replace those memories. It will be recalled that the elder Kean had fared no better in America several decades earlier. William Winter, who was to become Booth's chief exponent, gives another reason for the general antipathy that young Booth encountered in England— the strong British sentiment against "Yankees" in the early days of the Civil War.[5] As a matter of fact, the reception that the audience gave him can be considered kind; but the critics were cold. His supporting company of British players was likewise unresponsive. Some critics felt that Booth had contributed nothing of

---

[3] Edwin Booth edition, *The Merchant of Venice,* C. A. Alvard, New York, 1867, p. 9.

[4] *Boston Herald,* August 16, 1885.

[5] William Winter, *The Life and Art of Edwin Booth,* New York, 1894, p. 54.

distinction to the character, and in light of the manner in which he was yet to develop Shylock, it appears that this judgment was reasonably correct. He was lauded for his rich and sonorous voice, with its unusual range and flexibility, but there were criticisms of his uneven use of his mobile features and of his powerfully expressive eyes.

But the press, for the most part, found his conception thoughtful and consistent. It saw in Booth's Shylock, no vulgar Israelite, but a man so disappointed in his avarice and so gratified at the thought of revenge, that his utterance was choked when he attempted to express these sentiments. The critics conceded that his action in the trial scene was competent; they noted the contrast that Booth marked between Shylock's thirst for revenge and his humiliation at finding himself ruined and disgraced. They admitted that his final exit, with the picture of the suffering and silent Jew, was so well drawn that they were affected. But this praise was offered grudgingly. His portrayal of Richelieu, on the other hand, was regarded with enthusiasm. It was, incidentally, during this tour, that there appeared with him in Manchester in the role of Bassanio, a young actor who was to serve, for the remainder of Booth's career, as his strongest competitor for theatrical honors— Henry Irving.

Upon his return to the United States, Booth enjoyed an unusually happy five-year period, and the critics, more or less unanimously, pronounced him the finest actor of the day. The most detailed account of his performance, however, is a derogatory one, and very likely it reports his style quite accurately. The writer is disappointed to find that Booth's Shylock had

> . . . neither prudence of mien or moderation of tongue. When we remember how completely the Israelite was hedged in by prejudice; how narrow and slippery was the path he trod; how uncertain was his tenure of life, property, justice, anything, it becomes impossible to reconcile Mr. Booth's Shylock with the Jew of Shakespeare. . . . In these days . . . the fierce malignity and noise of his speech would consign him inevitably to the Station-house. . . . In the early days of Venice he would have been tossed from the Rialto into the canal. There were moments . . . when Mr. Booth positively ranted . . . and a stormy person threw his arms aloft and made night hideous. . . . Throughout the piece there was a constant effort to make the character

melodramatic. There is no reason why Shylock should hobble about the stage in the way he does. . . . Decrepitude in life is the loss of vital power; on the stage it is the occasion for displaying it. Mr. Booth's youth generally leads him to excesses in this respect. He forgets that all that is left to age is the fire of the brain. Let us rather say that he forgets it in this piece, for surely in Richelieu he remembers it distinctly. . . . But in Shylock it is senility without weakness; rage without purpose; noise without meaning. . . . It is in vain that we try to recall a memorable trait in Mr. Booth's interpretation. The loss of Jessica would have been effective if he had not already howled so much that trifles like the loss of a daughter had become unimportant to the audience. In the last act all the old miserable business of sharpening the knife was perpetuated with a minuteness that was wearisome.[6]

Edwin Forrest, who had in his day rivalled both Edmund Kean and the elder Booth, was a veteran of superb reputation when Edwin Booth came on the scene. Forrest displayed in his matured portrayal of Shylock the same individualization for which he was now noted in all his roles. His dramatization was developed out of a familiarity with the appearance, the language and the manners of the character, and evidently he analyzed his portrayal deeply. The Mirror had reported of his Shylock: ". . . not as a part put on for an hour, but as a being whom we have seen, and whose grievance we commiserated, and in whose revenge we took a part."[7] Yet for all of the thoughtfulness of Forrest's interpretation, he found a keen rival in young Booth. It was in the intellectual and spiritual qualities that Booth's methods were most sharply contrasted with those of Forrest. Forrest's delineation of Shylock was remembered for its fierce animal intensity, while Booth's acting eclipsed it with a method, for all its extravagance, that was basically simple—one that displayed the grotesquely tragic side of Shylock's personality. Forrest made no compromise in his acting of Shylock and finally, in his last years, he felt obliged to discard the role, as he had that of Iago, because of his distaste for a part in which he felt it necessary to awaken the loathing of his audience. His Shylock, among other things, carried a whetstone for sharpening

---

[6] *Times,* February 4, 1867.

[7] December 8, 1827.

his knife in the trial scene, and it is clear that Forrest aimed at sensationalism of the *grand guignol* variety.

As Edwin Booth matured in the role, his Shylock had no such diabolic proclivities. Unlike his father, he saw the Jew's predicament as primarily an economic one. The pangs that were felt by this younger Shylock were founded on his hatred of the rival merchant who interfered with his money-lending. It was for this, above all, that he sought revenge. Booth kept Shylock's racial hatred of the Christian distinct from his personal hatred of Antonio, "skilfully using the former in order to throw out in darker background the shadowy background of the latter."[8]

This business-like Shylock did not exhibit the religious frenzy of his predecessors; his Jewishness was scarcely apparent. He was, unlike his early portrayal of the role, predominately a man of cold and deadly bearing. In a letter to his friend, Furness, Booth sets down his reasons for his characterization: he is chiefly impressed by the meanness and corruptness of Shylock's nature. Shylock's avariciousness is evidenced by his response to the loss of Leah's ring; he is concerned only with its monetary value. Had he been a loving father, Jessica would not have deserted him. We are moved by a sense of pity for Shylock only because it is we who are compassionate and not because of any virtue in Shylock's disposition.[9]

The details of the development of the character are worked out with the care of one who is setting down a blueprint. When the actor first enters as Shylock it is

> . . . with slow, shuffling gait; restless, half-closed eyes, and the fingers of his disengaged hand (one holds his staff) ever moving, as if from the constant habit of feeling and caressing the ducats that are passing through them. Speak with a measured and gruff voice.[10]

In Shylock's first scene, when he would have Bassanio understand that Antonio "is sufficient," Booth writes: "Indicate by gesture (touch your palm or the purse you carry) *what* you mean. All this is spoken deliberately, not too slowly, and with an occasional shrug

---

[8] Note by Henry L. Hinton in Edwin Booth edition. *The Merchant of Venice*, New York, 1867, p. 10.

[9] Furness, Variorum edition, p. 384.

[10] *Ibid.*, for this and following notes on Booth's acting.

of the shoulders." On "How like a fawning publican . . .," Winter
tells us that Booth delivered the lines:

> If I can *catch* him once upon the hip,
> I will *feed* FAT the ancient *grudge* I bear him.

Here, we are told, "the hand clutches, rigidly as a claw, at the
word *catch,* and dashes its prey toward a devouring maw as the
idea of *feeding fat* upon it glances into the expression." "Cursed
be my tribe . . ." is delivered in a lower tone, "almost growled
sotto voce. Turning your back on Antonio as he enters, and pretending to be lost in calculation of your 'present store'." He turns,
with pretended surprise at Antonio's presence, uncovers and ad-
dresses him obsequiously, "but with a touch of irony in voice and
face." On "many a time and oft . . .," Booth pauses before turning
to Antonio and shows great self-restraint. He instructs the actor
to "turn slowly, and beginning with rising inflection of voice,
address Antonio reproachfully." When he admonishes Antonio for
calling him "dog," the line is delivered sarcastically, "with a pause
and a gulp before 'dog.' . . . Utter 'courtesies' with strong emphasis—looking up, as you 'bend low,' with a devilish grin into
Antonio's face." Booth tells us that Antonio should stand erect
here, "looking contemptuously at Shylock till the end, when he
moves, as if stung, a few paces from his position, to return and
angrily reply, but not too violently, yet sufficiently to cause Shylock
to pretend alarm and regret at the 'storm' he had raised." He dis-
cusses the bond "jocosely." Booth's advice is to "keep up this expression and chuckle until Bassanio interferes, then suddenly change
it to disappointed rage,—but only for a moment; then, at 'O father
Abram . . .' assume a look and tone of pity." When Shylock hears
Antonio prophesy that the Hebrew will turn Christian, he "grins
at it as a pleasant joke, and moving slowly up the stage, turns
as they exeunt, and looks after them with intense hatred."

Booth's Shylock is reported as having been ablaze with delirium
in the street scene, but the passions he displayed were governed
and directed. He was explosive and tumultuous in the scene with
Tubal. It was in the trial scene that he epitomized the grim, self-
centered, revengeful and implacable personality that he believed
was the essence of Shylock's character. In his later years, he did

not rant in this scene, but exhibited a diabolically crafty nature and a macabre humor. His acting was marked by

> . . . that awful composure of inherent evil which may be noted in the observant stillness of a deadly reptile, aware of its potency and in no haste, although unalterably determined, to make use of it.[11]

Booth describes Shylock's entrance: ". . . slowly, until in front of the Duke. Then bow to him. Show great deference to the Duke throughout the Scene, but to none else, except, of course, to Portia, while she seems to favor your suit." Booth notes in the use of the knife: "Whet the knife on the sole of the shoe,—not too rapidly." We are told that Booth crossed upstage at this point and very quietly prepared to take the pound according to his bond "without rant, fuss or fury." He warns against the danger of causing laughter by making a "gag" of the knife-sharpening business. Booth may not have heeded his own advice, for an interpolated note in an actor's prompt-book, attributes to Booth the ludicrous business of feeling the blade with his finger, and in order to test its sharpness, pulling a hair from his head and dropping it on the edge.[12]

There is nothing essentially unusual in Booth's handling of the trial scene, save its close. When he hears that he must relinquish his faith, he shrinks; "and at the word 'Christian' utters a short, sharp groan, staggers backward and raises his right hand with the palm upward—face also upraised, with a look of utter despair, until the Duke has spoken, then collapses. When Portia asks him 'Art thou contented . . .' Shylock raises both head and hands as if about to appeal to Portia, checks himself, and says very slowly, as head and hands drop, 'I am content.' His last words are uttered plaintively.[13] As Shylock is leaving, Gratiano seizes his left arm,

---

[11] Winter, *op. cit.,* p. 304.

[12] Moore's prompt-book, Folger Shakespeare Library.

[13] In his *Prefaces to Shakespeare,* Granville-Barker writes that it is a great error to make of the simplicity of the line, "I am not well," the occasion for an effective exit. By doing so, the remainder of the play becomes an anti-climax. (Princeton, 1946, p. 359 footnote.) Stoll believes that it is only our feeling of compassion that makes us sympathize with Shylock when we realize how much the spirit has gone out of him. Not a soul on the stage, however, feels pity for the Jew. That he is not well, probably provokes a laugh from them. (Elmer Edgar Stoll, "Shakespeare's Jew," *University of Toronto Quarterly,* January, 1939, pp. 139-154.)

and at the conclusion of the taunting speech . . . casts Shylock's hand from him. Shylock bows low to the Duke, and slowly totters towards the door,—he meets Antonio, and shrinks with abhorrence; raises his hand (as on previous occasions), which slowly descends upon the back of his head as it droops upon his breast,—falls against the door, which slowly opens. The Curtain should be 'timed' to Shylock's exit." This characterization was considered by the critics of the day, as being natural, smooth and spontaneous. It presented Shylock in what was thought to be his proper perspective—merely as a menace to the happiness of others. There seems to have been no dissatisfaction expressed by Booth's admirers for the way in which he left the Portia story unresolved.

These data concerning the production are to be found in Booth's notes, his prompt-books of the play and in his acting edition. This gives us an abbreviated four-act version that Booth employed through most of his years as Shylock. The play, which is made to end abruptly with the trial scene on the line, "To bring thee to the gallows, not the font," is in the tradition of many of his predecessors. The four-act version was the rule rather than the exception in this period. As early as 1836, when Andrew Campbell appeared as Shylock at Sadler's Wells, it had been advertised as "concluding with the trial scene." American audiences of Booth's generation had never seen Act V, and it remained the happy task of Ellen Terry, in Henry Irving's production, to present it for the first time.

Booth's direction left much to be desired. He showed restraint in not smothering the action of the street and trial scenes with excessive crowds of supernumeraries, as had Charles Kean, but for the most part, he was careless with artistic details. This relative indifference to staging became strongly apparent when Henry Irving's memorable version of the play was presented a decade later, but until that time, Booth was able to claim an uncontested place for his production of the play. If lovers of Shakespeare found insufficient pleasure in Booth's abrupt conclusion, they were compensated by the Petruchio that usually was played after it. This was perfect billing for Booth. In these two roles he could exhibit his talents in both tragedy and comedy, and in America no one questioned his claim that he was, at least, the foremost living tragic actor.

Booth's famous Winter Garden revival of *The Merchant of Venice* was presented as a picturesque pageant. The scenery, designed by Charles W. Witham, one of the outstanding architectural artists of his day, was modelled after the original pictures of streets and buildings in old Venice and showed the strong influence of Charles Kean's production. Odell says it was "probably as correct and magnificent as anything seen up to that time in America."[14] The costumes were rich and fine. Booth's Shylock was swathed in variegated Oriental draperies and Winter describes his grizzled hair, his red cap and the pointed red shoes that were considered to be proper trappings of a Jew. A colored engraving further shows this Shylock wearing a pointed and parted white beard, earrings, slouch hat, pouch purse, with numerous rings on his fingers and even on his thumbs.[15] The Booth edition of the play states that the costumes for the Jewish characters did not differ from those worn by the others in the play, except for the yellow bonnets. Apparently this similarity of costume was advocated but not practiced.[16]

Booth's career was crowded with many personal tragedies and consequently his performance was subject to a good deal of variation. During the illness of his first wife, Mary Devlin, Booth attempted to fulfill his engagements as usual. His failure must have been conspicuous, for at least one critic could not refrain from complaining about the way he was murdering Shakespeare.[17] Upon the death of his wife, Booth retired temporarily from the stage. He returned a half-year later, but the assassination of Lincoln by his brother, John Wilkes Booth, dealt him a paralyzing blow, and again he withdrew from the stage. When the Winter Garden was destroyed by fire, the theatrical equipment that Booth had accumulated over the years was lost. The man's hopes were destroyed as well, and the death of his second wife left Booth bereft of any

---

[14] *Annals of the New York Stage,* New York, 1936, vol. VIII, p. 149.

[15] Theatre Collection, Houghton Library, Harvard University.

[16] A note in Booth's acting edition cites Vecellio as his authority for the use of yellow head coverings, but here he was frankly borrowing from Charles Kean's source. The story of how a red-bonneted Jew was once mistaken for a Cardinal, and henceforth the edict to wear yellow hats was enforced, was an interesting one to publish, but on the stage, red was the more striking color.

[17] *Herald,* February 25, 1863.

desire to continue living. It is needless to point out the extent to
which his remaining years as an actor bore the ineradicable scars
of these calamities.

What Winter defends as vertigo, but Booth's less devoted critics
insisted was the result of alcoholism, had a marked effect on the
actor's mode of delivery. Even before the series of catastrophes had
begun to blight his art, he was criticized for his slovenly diction.
The vibrant tonal quality of his earliest days was replaced by a
strong nasal intonation that may have been an affectation of one
of his father's peculiarities. He had always had a tendency to slur
his lines except in his favorite scenes. As he grew older, his
articulation became increasingly sluggish—the outer manifestation
of a weary spirit. But there were few critical references to his loss
of dexterity, and apparently he kept his magic.

During the period that Booth and Irving simultaneously held
the boards as Shylock, one of the liveliest points of discussion in
theatrical circles concerned the question of which was the better
actor. The most discriminating opinions seemed to favor Booth for
his acting and Irving for his talent in surrounding himself with an
excellent supporting cast and with the ultimate refinements of
staging. Booth did not have the benefit of an Ellen Terry as
Portia, as Irving did through his long years as Shylock. He had,
indeed, co-starred with many competent Portias, among them Charlotte Cushman and Helena Modjeska, but even actresses of their
stature never achieved the unity and the breadth of conception that
only maturity in a role can bring.

While Booth's production continued to be showy and expensive,
it was marked by the effects of old-age when Irving brought his
production to America. Lawrence Barrett, who had played Bassanio
to Booth's Shylock with distinction for many years, and who was
soon to serve as still another Shylock competitor in a six-act version
of the play, was now middle-aged. In comparison with the Bassanio
of William Terriss of Irving's company, he suffered considerably.
None of the many black-robed Portias who played the role with
Booth was a match for the captivating scarlet-gowned young judge
of Ellen Terry. As for Booth, as ardent an admirer as Odell recalls
his lack of strength in the trial scene at this time, attributing it
to the fact that "he had been through too much." The time for
his retirement was approaching, and *The Times,* not very subtly,

reminded its readers of the youthful age at which Garrick had left the stage.[18]

Although he was deeply admired in Germany, Booth did not fare much better in London than he did in America during this period. One English critic deplored the fact that Booth had attempted the role of Shylock at all on this occasion; he was not in the vein:

> He was acting; but not feeling the character. He was mechanically correct; but artistically false. He astonished and amazed the ignorant when he was most untrue; but he persuaded or influenced very few. In his rage there was no fierceness of invective; in his lament no ring of pathos. The disappointment with Tubal was petulance; and no tortured soul spoke with those immortal lines — 'no satisfaction, no revenge . . . no tears but of my shedding'. All was unsatisfactory as an echo; all as hollow as a grave. And no change of material consequence came with the Trial Scene. Words there were on the topmost froth of thought, but no proper or safe guidance to show what manner of man this Shylock was. The actor assisted the scene; but he did not fill it.[19]

It is clear that the critic's dissatisfaction was only with Booth's Shylock. Portia was reported as having considerable verve and dramatic impulse, while the account of Booth's Petruchio, which followed on the bill, was altogether laudatory.

Meanwhile theatrical practice was changing with great rapidity. The custom since the days of Colley Cibber of admitting play-goers to the theatre later in the evening at half-price, at long last went out of style. In the past, spectators who had purchased full tickets had normally been refunded a portion of the admission charge if they did not wish to remain for the pantomime that followed the major presentation. The result was the gradual elimination of the multiple bill. The curtain-time had been slowly advanced through the years. Quaint as the verse that appeared on an 1822 play-bill now seemed, its inclusion, at the time, was a serious attempt to assure the adventurous play-goer of his safety:

> Let none be afraid from the country to come,
>   As the moon is engaged to light you safe home;

[18] Cited by Odell, *Annals of the New York Stage*, New York, 1945, vol. XIV, p. 541.

[19] *Illustrated London News*, March 26, 1881.

But should she herself that high honour decline, —
The stars have agreed with new lustre to shine;
Doors open at six, to begin about seven, —
At home, safe in bed, betwixt ten and eleven.[20]

Eating habits, too, were changing, and the trend toward opening the theatre after the dinner hour in the evening slowly asserted itself. These departures from age-old theatrical tradition gave rise to a series of new practices. The matinee system came into existence. In addition, Saturday morning performances, particularly by the leading actors who were on tour, were offered, largely for the patronage of women and school children.

The Jewish question was also becoming more marked in America, which was by no means free from anti-Jewish prejudice in the period following the Civil War. A number of journalists found opportunity for the expression of anti-Semitic sentiments in the Shylock story. One writer, in reviewing Booth's first performance at the Winter Garden, spoke of "that unquenchable lust of lucre which marks the race," and used the dramatic column for a bit of editorializing:

It is true, that money-changers once spat on in the ghetto are now hugged in the palace. Rothschilds and Goulds, Belmonts and Benjamins are found in ante-chambers of princes and of presidents. But we fear that it is not so much that the prejudice against the Jews has ceased but that the love of money has increased — not that the Jews have become as Christians, but that Christians have become as Jews. . . .

The manly quality of revenge, explains the writer, is not a Jewish characteristic:

Shakespeare might have ransacked every ghetto in Christendom without finding a Jew who would have preferred a pound of Flesh to a pound sterling. . . . Jews also shrink from physical contests. Their disposition is to triumph by cunning and intellect rather than violence. . . .[21]

Such opinions continued to be characteristic of post-Civil War America. As late as 1877, Joseph Seligman, to whom President

---

[20] Performance of *The Merchant of Venice; or The Cruel Jew,* at Theatre-Royal, Worcester, December 26, 1822, Stead Collection.

[21] Unidentified clipping in Edwin Booth prompt-book, Folger Shakespeare Library.

Grant, possibly in an attempt to compensate for his infamous Order Number 11[22] of Civil War days, had offered the post of Secretary of the Treasury, was denied admittance to Judge Hilton's Grand Union Hotel in Saratoga Springs on religious grounds. The incident resulted in a considerable stir. Seligman's banking firm had, in large measure, financed the Civil War by obtaining European capital for Lincoln. It had later become the financial agency of the Navy Department. The Grand Union affair evoked energetic disapproval in many quarters, and particularly from the pulpit of Henry Ward Beecher. The collapse of A. T. Stewart's in Philadelphia, which was then under the management of Judge Hilton, and later taken over by John Wanamaker, was said to be a direct outcome of the Grand Union incident. The fate of Shakespeare's Jew, for woe or for weal, was not regarded by American theatre-goers at this time as without contemporary significance.

The tendency toward Jew-baiting in the United States in this period naturally found its expression in the theatre. A long series of Shylock burlesques caught the public fancy, and further capital was made of this tendency in the presentation of a number of farces that dramatized the Jew unfavorably. The most extravagant of these was entitled *Jew Trouble at Manhattan Beach*,[23] an attraction upon which everything but good taste was lavished. Large advertisements in the daily newspapers during the 1878-79 season, announcing this play with a cast of one-hundred at Pastor's Theatre in New York, linked it unmistakably with the "Christians only" attitude that had given rise to the Grand Union affair.

It was during this period that Booth finally discontinued his practice of ending the play with Shylock's last exit. Sufficient energy broke through his seeming inertia for him to restore, at this late date, the end of Act IV as well as the complete fifth act in which Modjeska could display her talent. His acting version now was the one being used by Lawrence Barrett in his production.

---

[22] Two orders were issued over General Grant's signature, on November 9 and 10, 1862, instructing subordinates to refuse all permits to go south, especially to Jews, and ordering conductors on the railroads to allow no Jew to travel southward. This was followed by Order Number 11, on December 17, issued by an assistant adjutant-general, supposedly at Grant's behest, expelling all Jews from his department. On January 7, 1863, the order was revoked by General Halleck, general-in-chief at that time.

[23] By George L. Stout and Alfred Trumble.

This inclusion was undoubtedly the result of the rivalry he encountered in the success of other companies, rather than any conviction as to its efficacy. The race between Booth and Irving continued unabated. Play-goers who frequented Haverly's Brooklyn Theatre in the 1884 season saw Booth as Shylock one week and Irving in the same role the following week. We are impressed by the popularity of the play during this period. Irving had appeared in *The Merchant of Venice* at the same theatre but two months earlier. The competition was a friendly one; at the height of his career, Irving played Iago to Booth's Othello in a London engagement triumphant for both.

Booth's attempts to keep abreast of current trends in staging never halted. The music and the dance program that was woven into the script became more and more elaborate as time went on. Toward the end of his career, as many as ten selections were presented during the course of the play, in a masque, the music for which was written by Sir Arthur Sullivan. Booth continued to work for scenic and historic fidelity at the time when his contemporaries were making great strides in staging, but he was finally outdone by Irving, the one actor whose productions were superior to his and whose study of Shylock was to be regarded by the leading American critics as being the profoundest interpretation any actor had ever given to Shakespeare's Jew.

HENRY IRVING as SHYLOCK
Brander Matthews Dramatic Museum, Columbia University

CHAPTER V

Henry Irving

A CONSIDERATION of the contributions made to the theatre by the great actors of the past leads to the conclusion that many of them merely imitated the characterizations of their forerunners. The history of a role is usually a static account. In general, the actor displays his craft by carrying on an established tradition. His treatment of a part is often the result of the elaboration of detail, but of few significant changes. We can enumerate relatively few names of the actors whose reputations were founded primarily on innovation.

When in 1856, an eighteen-year-old boy called Henry Brodribb first faltered through the lines of Salarino and Bassanio, there was little promise of the exciting days that were to follow for Henry Irving. It was under this stage name, acquired fifteen years after his first appearance, that the greatest of all Shylocks learned, not to break with tradition, but to select only those elements that would crystallize his characterization of the role. Irving played Shylock eight years after he undertook the dual role of actor-producer of *The Bells*. *The Merchant of Venice* was Irving's second Shakespearean presentation; his *Hamlet* had met with but moderate success. He had absorbed much of the new spirit of stage management—for which he was deeply indebted to Edward W. Godwin—but he could hardly have expected the sensation he produced when he brought the curtain down on the *Merchant of Venice* in London's Royal Lyceum Theatre on November 1, 1879.

Irving came to the theatre with few endowments, indeed. His family was not connected with the stage, and he had changed his name to avoid casting a slur upon it by his choice of profession. Nor was he generously equipped by nature. Thin, ungraceful, of

79

medium height, he affected an ungainly angular carriage and a
stride that caricaturists later became fond of emphasizing. But
somehow he managed to make his five feet, nine and a half inches
appear to tower over the stage. To compensate for a weak and
often inaudible voice, he had to acquire a forced nasal quality of
production. His "cut-thrut-dug" and similar divagations from standard pronunciation were noted with dismay. There was frequent
praise by the critics for the perfection of delivery of every member
of the company but Irving. According to Max Beerbohm, he never
could master the true music and magic of Shakespeare's verse,[1]
although he could teach others to read beautifully. While his voice
remained, throughout his life, hopelessly out of tune, his subtle
and intellectually satisfying readings stood out in sharp contrast to
the less thoughtful renditions of most of the actors of his day. That
he could not flex his talents and therefore had to make all of his
own mannerisms seem to suit the characters he portrayed, that
neither his voice, face, figure nor carriage were transformable; in
short, that he could not impersonate—to all this there is ample
testimony. He was not versatile. Nevertheless, his personality tran-
scended his lack of physical endowment. He had intense personal
magnetism. His limitations obviously fitted him only for eccentric
characters of a melodramatic turn. Doubtless, it was his limitations
as well as his genius that led him to select and magnify the role
of Shylock.

Irving's *The Merchant of Venice* was the first thorough-going
effort to stage Shakespeare's play in a period-setting of beauty and
authenticity. His obligation, as he saw it, was to represent the work
with strict fidelity to Shakespeare's intention, and although some
of the critics were loud in their denial that his Shylock was
Shakespeare's Jew, they were quick to recognize the infinite care
that had been given each detail and the spirit of consistency and
appropriateness that marked his production. Irving rejected the time-
honored practice of trimming the play down in order to make it a
starring vehicle. Although he eliminated the Prince of Arragon role
that had been restored by Charles Kean and though he cut the
scenes between Jessica, Lorenzo and Launcelot immediately following Portia's departure from Belmont, he re-introduced the rarely-

---

[1] *Around Theatres*, New York, 1930, pp. 512-513.

acted jailer scene and the casket scenes in full. Most important was his restoration of the long deleted fifth act in all of its moonlit loveliness.

Odell calls Irving's presentation

> . . . perhaps the most perfect Shakespearean production we have ever seen. . . . Venice lived again before us, thanks to Irving's scene-painters and costumers, as we had dreamed of it. The management of the crowds, the masquing revellers, on the night of Shylock's going forth, the bridges, the palaces, the gondolas, all were there. . . .[2]

The Herald concurs with Odell in its comments on this same production:

> . . . nothing more admirable than the stage arrangement of this play can well be conceived. It is not so much the opulence of the costumes, the picturesqueness of the groupings, or the beauty of the scenery which makes of this production a triumph of stage art, as the taste, the discretion, the poetic tact with which they are applied. Never at any moment is there . . . excess of illustration . . . but all the stage adjuncts . . . cooperate to give an air of vraisemblance to the whole, to localize the story and to produce an effective background for the principal actors.[3]

If Irving accomplished nothing more than the creation of a complete effect for the play, he is deserving of the aura that surrounds his name. Some of his predecessors had indeed directed their efforts toward correctly-dressed and properly-mounted stage productions. He was not the first to mount the play well. He was widely praised for the wonderful effect he gained by the use of a practicable bridge over the canal in Act III, but as we have seen in this regard, he was merely carrying on the tradition of Charles Kean, who had introduced the functional bridge in 1858. But Kean had never achieved a unity of effect like that of Irving. Irving's production left an impression of sheer magic; it was the perfect marriage of text and showmanship.

In the prefatory note to his acting version, Irving writes:

> In producing *The Merchant of Venice* I have endeavored to avoid hampering the natural action of the piece with any

---

[2] *Annals of the New York Stage,* New York, 1940, vol. XII, p. 227.

[3] November 7, 1883.

unnecessary embellishment; but have tried not to omit any
accessory which might heighten the effects.[4]

His friend and biographer, Austin Brereton, while lauding the
general effectiveness of the production as a "revelation," has little
beyond this to say of its scenic wonders. He attributes its overwhelming success, rather, to Irving's intelligent and admirable
acting.[5] Odell confesses that his personal recollection is not one
of the staging, but of Irving's delineation of "a very human
Shylock."[6] It is with this characterization that we are chiefly
concerned.

Most impressive in Irving's presentation is the apparent freshness
with which he approached the Shylock role. He seems to have
discarded all the interpretations of his contemporaries. He wrote
in his *Impressions of America*:

> I look on Shylock as the type of a persecuted race; almost
> the only gentleman in the play and the most ill-used. He
> is a merchant, who trades in the Rialto, and Bassanio and
> Antonio are not ashamed to borrow money of him, nor to
> carry off his daughter. The position of his child is more or
> less, a key to his own. She is a friend of Portia. Shylock
> was well-to-do — a Bible-read man . . . and there is nothing
> in his language, at any time, that indicates the snuffling
> usurer.[7]

His characterization was apparently studied from the life. Robert
Hichins quotes Irving as having said, "I took many ideas for my
Shylock from a Moorish Jew I saw when I was yachting once
and went ashore in Morocco. They were astounding fellows."[8] As
his production matured, he was not content to standardize his
own creation. It was organic. In her autobiography, Ellen Terry
describes Irving's practice of constantly revising his reading of
Shylock.[9] The critics of his day were as quick to discern his
changes as Irving was to keep his Shylock from becoming static.

---

[4] Irving edition, London, 1880.

[5] *The Life of Henry Irving*, London, 1908.

[6] Odell, *op. cit.*, vol. XIII, 1942), p. 431.

[7] Henry Irving, *Impressions of America*, London, 1884, p. 265f.

[8] H. A. Saintsbury and Cecil Palmer (eds.), *We Saw Him Act*, London,
1939, p. 166.

[9] *The Story of My Life*, London, 1908, p. 186.

Unhappily, his alterations were not always indicative of his intellectual integrity, but rather of the tenor of audience reaction. He was, after all, an actor.

At first Irving evidently conceived Shylock

> . . . as a representative of a race which generation after generation has been cruelly used, insulted, execrated. It is an hereditary hate, but to this as the play progresses are added individual wrongs that make him inexorable and fiendish.[10]

It was a study of what man becomes in a stupid and oppressive environment. *The Theatre* finds Irving's Shylock distinguished by his dignity:

> He feels and acts as one of a noble but long oppressed nation. In point of all intelligence and culture he is far above the Christians with whom he comes in contact, and the fact that as a Jew he is deemed far below them in the social scale, is gall and wormwood to his proud and sensitive spirit.[11]

Hawkins describes Irving's Shylock as

> . . . a picturesque figure with an air of a man feeling the bitterness of oppression, and conscious of his own superiority in all but circumstance to the oppressor — a feeling which is finely indicated when, in talk with Antonio, he touches the Christian merchant, and, seeing the action resented, bows deprecatingly with an affectation of deep humility.[12]

Hichins has a somewhat different interpretation. Irving's Jew was no doubt often repulsive

> . . . but he had moments of sheer humanity, when one felt with him, and almost, or quite, suffered with him. Something of the eternal man, subject to the striving and suffering which is the common lot of all human beings, pierced through the crust of his greedy Jewishness, prey-demanding, revengeful, and bitter, and went to the heart. One almost forgave him.[13]

---

[10] *Herald,* November 7, 1883.

[11] December, 1879.

[12] *Saturday Review,* November 8, 1879.

[13] Saintsbury and Palmer, *op. cit.,* p. 166.

The England of 1879 was not deeply involved in any consideration of a "Jewish problem." Many of the more modern literary
critics have expressed the belief that Shakespeare intended a plea
for toleration that stemmed from the excitement caused by the
alleged iniquities of Dr. Lopez. But whatever Shakespeare's intention
was, the Victorians were prepared to accept the Shylock Irving gave
them, a Shylock marked by intense pathos and a keen sense of
injury. Nevertheless, Hichins relates that

> . . . he went out like a broken man, who . . . by will
> power and because he knew many eyes were watching
> him, managed to keep some shreds of dignity, like rags to
> hide nakedness, about him.[14]

Doubtless, this Shylock was a revelation for the playgoer of 1879.

Dignity was the keynote of the opening performance, although
the 7:30 curtain-raiser, Pinero's *Daisy's Escape,* billed as an "original
comedietta," with the playwright doubling as actor, could scarcely
be considered an appropriate forerunner. First-nighters could pur-
chase Irving's acting version of *The Merchant of Venice* in the theatre for one shilling, but little did the audience realize what it was
about to witness. This Shylock appeared to be between fifty and
sixty years of age; he was infirm enough to be supported by a cane.
He wore an iron-gray wisp of beard, a brown gabardine girdled with
an Oriental shawl and a close-fitting black cap with a yellow line
across it. Nothing in his physical appearance, save its sedate quality,
gave hint of the tone of his performance. The theme was revenge,
but this Shylock was an extraordinary man. Irving not only gave him
stature and dignity, but also transformed him from antagonist to
protagonist, shifted sympathy to him and also focused attention
upon his wrong. For the first time, Shylock took his place among
the great figures of tragedy. The fact that he played in a comedy
was something else again.

In Irving's conception, the vengence theme in *The Merchant of
Venice* becomes completely clear. There can be no doubt of how this
Shylock plotted the bond business: he planned his revenge from
the moment he asked Antonio to go to the notary to sign the bond.
Antonio is disarmed of any suspicion by Shylock's seeming indifference and his indication that he would gain nothing of value in obtaining his pound of flesh. Irving notes that the speech, "Go with

---

[14] *Ibid.,* p. 167.

me to a notary . . . ," must be given with deliberate hurriedness. The same air of assumed frankness and good nature that characterize the conclusion of Shylock's preceding speech, "I would be friends with you . . . ," should be continued, while the words are delivered rapidly, since he does not wish to give Antonio or Bassanio time to dwell on the conditions of the contract.[15]

The Spectator depicts Irving's Shylock as a man "whom none can despise, who can raise emotion both of pity and of fear, and make us Christians thrill with a retrospective sense of shame."[16] It was undoubtedly the poignancy of this Shylock that evoked such a flood of praise for Irving. William Winter saw the Jew as austere, inveterate of purpose, vindictive, cruel, ruthless—but human. He tells us that unlike his predecessors, Irving's tone was not one of raving, but of intense passion "that can hardly speak."[17]

The two scenes singled out most frequently by the critics for distinction are those of Shylock's return after Jessica's elopement and the trial scene. Ellen Terry, whose Portia "thoroughly fascinated if she did not convince"[18] audiences through most of the twenty-six years of Irving's sensational run of a thousand performances writes that "for absolute pathos, achieved by absolute simplicity of means, I never saw anything in the theatre to compare with his Shylock's returning home after Jessica's flight."[19] *The Herald* describes Irving's original stage-business—Shylock returning from the banquet through the darkened streets that a few minutes before had been ablaze with light and mirth, knocking at his door, to find himself robbed and deserted by his daughter; the unrelieved simplicity of Irving's characterization as he stands there, waiting, waiting, while the curtain slowly descends.[20] Winter remembers "the image of the father convulsed with grief momentarily but sincerely."[21]

The Saturday Review commends Irving for introducing a fine touch of invention. He has Lorenzo fleeing with Jessica and her

---

[15] Irving edition, note 101.

[16] November 8, 1879.

[17] *Shadows of the Stage,* New York, 1892, p. 183.

[18] *Herald,* November 7, 1888.

[19] Terry, *op. cit.,* p. 186.

[20] November 7, 1883.

[21] Winter, *op. cit.,* p. 182.

stolen money, the carnival crowds of masquers crossing the stage and disappearing over the picturesque bridge with laughter and music—"then Shylock is seen, lantern in hand, advancing, bent in thought; and, as he comes close to his robbed and deserted house the curtain falls." Here the critic halts in his praise to suggest that the effect would be doubled if the curtain had not fallen for a moment and been raised again just before this appearance of Shylock. He finds Shylock "less vehement here than may be expected . . . the Jew's passion seems to have exhausted him, but it is not the less intense in itself. He is overweighted with trouble."[22]

Hichins lauds Irving's ability in this instance to impress an audience with his utter stillness. He writes:

> It was an absolutely silent scene. One simply saw the figure of the Jew in the shadows walking slowly and alone to his house. But who that saw that figure can ever forget it?[23]

The speech that concludes with "no tears but of my shedding" was of particular interest to the critics. The writer in *The Saturday Review* says it was "charged with the pathos of the heaviest grief."[24] Winter records, not very informatively, that with these lines, Irving's Shylock took a strong clutch upon the emotions and created an effect that would never be forgotten.[25] There are one or two dissenting votes, of course. *The Saturday Review* account of the opening night critically notes that Irving's acting of Shylock, bewailing the loss of his daughter and his ducats, was at variance with the rest of the performance. He exhibited a loss of dignity here that destroyed, by this instance of over-acting, the symmetry he had achieved in the rest of the play.[26] Irving's constant awareness of the critics and his eagerness to reconcile his interpretation with their notions is demonstrated by the report that he at once altered his manner in this scene.

One is impressed by the intelligence of the critical reviews during this period. Points that would ordinarily receive little attention in

---

[22] November 8, 1879.

[23] Saintsbury and Palmer, *op. cit.,* p. 168.

[24] November 8, 1879.

[25] Winter, *op. cit.,* p. 183.

[26] November 8, 1879.

our contemporary press were carefully considered, appreciated and debated. Joseph Knight calls Irving's Shylock too restless in the scene with Tubal; "the violent shaking of the head and one or two similar things suggesting snappishness rather than passion."[27] The writer admits that his censure here may be churlish, considering the advance made by Irving over former representation, as well as the public's enthusiastic reception of the performance. The writer in *The Saturday Review* feels that the intensity of the last portion of the speech relegates the reference to Leah's ring to relative insignificance.[28] Several seasons later, *The Herald* noted Irving's revision of this scene: "he abandoned himself to a perfect tempest of passion that carried all before it."[29]

The discrepancies that may exist between the preconceptions of the critic and the intentions of the actor are often very great but not always measurable. It is only when we encounter the rare actor who records his plan of interpretation, that we have concrete evidence of his intention and a means of evaluating criticism. Such a body of evidence is to be found in the Irving and Marshall notes to *The Merchant of Venice*.[30] They illustrate the deep search for meaning that underlay all of Irving's readings. In "Why look you, how you storm," Irving insists that it is not Antonio, but Shylock who storms. But suddenly conscious of his error in losing his temper, because he has already a plan of vengeance, he now assumes an air of injured innocence, as if to show that he has been misunderstood all along. "This speech," advises Irving, "should be given with a well-acted air of *bonhommie*." In the opening lines of the jailer scene, Shylock's malicious merriment stands in sharp contrast, Irving explains, to the tragic rage he exhibits in the scene with Tubal. He must appear for a time to have forgotten the loss of his daughter. We have a key to the heroic quality of the trial scene when Irving recommends that Shylock's demeanor here be more dignified than

---

[27] Joseph Knight, *Theatrical Notes,* London, 1893, p. 304.

[28] November 8, 1879.

[29] November 7, 1883.

[30] *The Works of William Shakespeare,* edited by Henry Irving and Frank A. Marshall, New York, 1890, vol. III.

before. His immovable resolution, although, in a bad cause, must be exhibited here.[31]

Some critics found inconsistencies in Irving's sympathetic portrayal of Shylock as a human being who had turned vindictive and cruel. They approved of the effect of the early part of the trial scene, when Irving's quiet and calm fixity showed the persistence of his resolution, but *The Saturday Review* noted the bitterness of the subdued scorn injected into "Signior Antonio, many a time and oft . . . ;" the diabolical mockery of good humor with which he proposes the "merry sport;" the hatred and desire for revenge so strongly marked in the resolution to go forth to supper "to feed upon the prodigal Christian."[32]

Odell recalls the imposing arrangement of the trial scene; the magnificoes, clothed in scarlet and ermine robes of state, seated on the right, the excited crowds, the scarlet-clad Portia contrasted with Shylock's somber Oriental garb. It stamped upon him "an indelible impression."[33] Of Shylock himself, *The Saturday Review* has "no room for anything but admiration. . . . He is the very incarnation of deadly, restless hatred." As Shylock listens to the Duke's speech

> . . . he has the horrible stillness and fascination of the rattle-snake. When he answers, his speech is that of a man possessed of his purpose, coldly tenacious of his rights. His object has been gained, and the passion which has been concentrated on it will not deign to waste itself in supporting a position that is unassailable. His scorn of Gratiano's railings seem bitter from habit, and not because he is one whit moved by them. There is something appalling in his aspect when he stands waiting for the long desired moment with the knife in one hand and the scales in the other, and his pointing to the bond with the knife as he asks 'Is it so nominated in the bond'? . . . When the moment of defeat arrives, it strikes him like lightning, but the effect, like

---

[31] There are underscored in one of Irving's prompt-books, and rewritten in the interleafings, as if to impress themselves more emphatically upon the actor, four phrases of Shylock's trial scene speeches. These reiterations tell more of the mood of doggedness that Irving expresses in the courtroom than any explication can convey: "I would have my bond;" "I stand for judgment;" I stand here for law;" "I stay here on my bond." Folger Shakespeare Library.

[32] November 8, 1879.

[33] *Shakespeare from Betterton to Irving*, New York, 1920, vol. II, p. 143.

that of his expected triumph, is so powerful that it cannot find expression in any accustomed use of gesture or attitude. He is still in his despair as in his victory; but it is the stillness of one suffering instead of threatening death. Where he before inspired terror, he cannot now but command respect for the very awfulness of his downthrow. He leaves the court with a dignity that seems the true expression of his belief in his nation and himself. His mind is occupied with greater matters than the light jeers of Gratiano, and to these jeers he replies with three slow downward movements of the head, which are infinitely expressive of his acceptance of that which has befallen him and of his power to bear himself nobly under its weight. Gratiano speaks an infinite deal of nothing, and what he says at that moment seems empty indeed when answered with this silent eloquence. Nothing could be finer than Mr. Irving's acting at this point.[34]

The Spectator depicts Shylock in the courtroom:

. . . standing almost motionless, his hands hanging by his sides — they are an old man's hands, feeble, except when passion turns them into gripping claws, and then that passion subsides into the quivering of age, which is like palsy — his gray, worn face, lined and hollow, mostly averted from the speakers who move him not; except when a gleam of murderous hate, suddenly and deadly, like the flash from a pistol, goes over it, and burns for a moment in the tired, melancholy eyes! Such a gleam there came when Shylock answered Bassanio's palliative commonplace, with 'Hates any man the thing he would not kill'? At the wretched jibes of Gratiano, and the amiable maunderings of the Duke, the slow, cold smile, just parting the lips and touching their curves, as light touches polished metal, passes over the lower part of the face, but it does not touch the eyes or lift the brow. This is one of Mr. Irving's most remarkable facial effects, for he can pass it through all the phases of a smile, up to surpassing sweetness. . . . He is wonderfully weird . . . it is impressive, never fantastic, — sometimes solemn and terrible. There was a moment when, as he stood, in the last scene, with folded arms and bent head, the very image of exhaustion, a victim, entirely convinced of the justice of his cause, he looked like a Spanish

---

[34] November 8, 1879.

painter's *Ecce Homo*. The likeness passed in an instant, for the next utterance is: —

> 'My deeds upon my head. I crave the law,
> The penalty and forfeit of my bond.'[35]

Lena Ashwell remembers the startling impression he made as Antonio said:

> Two things provided more, that for this favor
> He presently become a Christian.

"Irving simply looked up and there flashed to us the terrible punishment this meant, the tragic history and the agony of this stubborn race in their resistance to the Christian faith."[36] To heighten this effect, Irving introduced a crowd of Jews among the spectators on the stage. Their interest in Shylock was apparent throughout the trial scene. Odell tells us how they laughed at his mordant jests, hung on to Portia's words and despaired over the final decision of the court.[37] Knight describes Shylock's reaction to the idea of conversion, as that of an intolerable insult, while the eager knot of interested Jews received the news as they would have reacted to a striking thunderbolt.[38] Granville-Barker takes exception to the inclusion of Jewish sympathizers in the courtroom and is, in effect, critical of Irving's intention when he writes: "How any producer can bring himself so to discount the poignant sight of that drab, heroic figure, lonely amid the magnificence around, passes understanding!"[39]

Then came the final exit. *The Spectator* calls it the finest acting in the scene and describes ". . . the quiet shrug, the glance of ineffable, unfathomable contempt at the exulting booby, Gratiano . . . the expression of defeat in every limb and feature, the deep, gasping sigh, as he passes slowly out . . ."[40] Robert Hichins writes of that last speech of Shylock, "I am not well," "the whole misery of the impotent Jew's heart seemed to be conveyed to me in those four simple words."[41] Here we have the essence of Irving's Shylock. Over-

---

[35] November 8, 1879.

[36] Saintsbury and Palmer, *op. cit.,* pp. 328-329.

[37] *Shakespeare from Betterton to Irving,* vol. II, p. 423.

[38] *Theatrical Notes,* p. 303.

[39] *Prefaces to Shakespeare,* Princeton, 1946, p. 359, footnote.

[40] November 8, 1879.

[41] Saintsbury and Palmer, *op. cit.,* p. 166.

shadowing his threefold role of usurer, outraged father and vengeful creditor, is the haunting figure of a retreating, broken old man. For the first time in the long varied history of the character, the sympathy of the general audience had been enlisted and secured.

Counter-balancing the praise, however, is Henry James' assessment of Irving during that first theatrical season in London:

> Of his Shylock during last winter, it was often said that it presents his faults in their mildest and his merits in their highest form. In this there is possibly a great deal of truth; his representation of the rapacious and rancorous Jew has many elements of interest. He looks the part to a charm, or rather, we should say, to a repulsion, and he might be painted as he stands. His conception of it is a sentimental one, and he has endeavoured to give us a sympathetic, and above all, a pathetic Shylock. . . . The actor struck us as rigid and frigid, and above all as painfully behind the stroke of the clock. The deep-welling malignity, the grotesque horror, the red-hot excitement of the long-baffled, sore-hearted member of a despised trade, who has been all his life at a disadvantage, and who at last finds his hour and catches his opportunity — these elements had dropped out. Mr. Irving's Shylock is neither excited nor exciting, and many of the admirable speeches, on his lips, lack much of their incision; notably that outbreak of passion and prospective revenge after he finds that Antonio has become forfeit, and that his daughter has fled from him, carrying off her dowry. The great speech, with its grim refrain: "Let him look to his bond!" rising each time with an intenser pitch and culminating in a pregnant menace, this superb opportunity is missed; the actor, instead of being "hissing hot," as we have heard Edmund Kean described at the same moment, draws the scene out and blunts all its points.[42]

Winter, among others, noted the vast changes in interpreting Shylock as Irving played him through the years. The early humanitarian treatment eventually became coarsened. The reading was now marked by the sneer of loathing in "How like a *fawning* publican he looks;" the peculiar long, soft emphasis of "I *hate* him . . . ;" the contempt and scorn of "But more . . . money gratis" and "Let-him-look-to-his bond;" the cruelty of "On *what* compulsion *must* I?" These are illustrative of the bravura acting that Irving was now

---

[42] Henry James, *The Scenic Art, Notes on Acting and the Drama, 1872-1901,* New Brunswick, 1948, p. 140f.

affecting and of the characterization that left a lasting impression on many of his observers. Oscar Wilde, in a sonnet to Ellen Terry, referred to Shylock as the "accursed Jew."[43]

Irving's Shylock grew older; it is not clear that he matured, and there is evidence that he grew less subtle as time went on. Changes in his character are described as the placing of inordinate stress on the picturesque feature of the delineation. It almost certainly must have been a far cry from the 1879 days, for one critic finds Irving's portrayal exaggerated and grotesque, almost a caricature. He believes that "a stronger artist would attain higher results by finer processes and more subtle suggestion." He finds this an exaggerated but superficial treatment of Shylock, "where hate and fury border on mania. . . . The set passion for revenge resembles the rather futile rage of an epileptic peddler . . . not the stern resolve of a fateful avenger."[44] One might suspect a lack of objectivity in this writer's report, were it not that other reviewers express a similar opinion of Irving's Shylock at this time.

A new development in social-political England suggests a reason for this revised conception. It was the dawn of an era that was marked by fanatical nationalism. The tendency of the Jews to live and to act together as a homogeneous group, again set them apart as aliens. The ancient dislike for the non-conformist arose at the very time that the economic and political status of Jews was assured. Irving's newer characterization seemed to coincide with this trend. At least, he was now returning to the task nearest his heart— that of being a good showman.

Perhaps for the same reason, Irving eventually undid his achievement in reinstating Act V. It may be noted from the playbills that in 1880, the program for the one hundred and ninety-third performance of the initial production at the Lyceum has the play ending, for the first time, with the trial scene. There is neither apology nor explanation; the program for the performance offers the synopses of only the first four acts, quite as if they comprised the play's entirety. Irving may have thought that the second part of the program, which presented the premiere of the one-act idyll, *Iolanthe,*[45]

---

[43] *McClure's Magazine,* May, 1908.

[44] *New York Mirror,* January 7, 1888.

[45] Adapted by W. G. Wills from Henrik Herz' poem, *King Rene's Daughter.*

in which both he and Ellen Terry appeared furnished a mood similar to that created by the newly-deleted fifth act of Shakespeare. It is even more likely that by this time Irving was beginning to see himself as the central figure about whom all the interest in the play revolved, and that he finally discarded the conviction that Act V was necessary to the play. It had become a tragedy; and the tragedy ends with Act IV, although we must agree with Margaret Webster that Irving's dragging, broken exit from the courtroom, while it surely must have been touching, was a distortion of Shakespeare.[46] At any rate, Irving in the end was content to sacrifice the mood he had so magnificently developed, in favor of the acclaim he received for his individual performance. The play had become a vehicle and from this time on he was able to do with or without the fifth act, as mood or policy prompted him.

So much has been written concerning Irving as a producer that one is given the impression that much of his success as Shylock was dependent on his excellent supporting cast and on his magnificent staging of The Merchant of Venice. This is certainly not in accord with the facts. After his reputation had been firmly established as the greatest Shylock, Irving frequently presented an evening's program consisting of the trial scene and several other isolated scenes from plays he had produced. Such variety programs were great favorites of his audiences, and although they had little reference to his early ambition to present a play as a unified piece, they met with great approval. We find him, for example, accommodating his New York public with a farewell night performance of the trial scene, and in addition, Act IV of Louis XI, Act III of Charles I and the Cathedral scene from Much Ado About Nothing.[47] For actors' funds and benefits, Irving and Ellen Terry appeared many times during their careers in the trial scene. It had become a piece of bravura.

Another instance of Irving's departure from his original idea of presenting the play in an appropriate setting is to be found in a

[46] Shakespeare Without Tears, New York, 1942, p. 195. (See footnote, 13, p. 70.)

[47] March 26, 1884.

somewhat unusual performance at West Point.[48] The actor who played Lorenzo records the event:

> This was great fun. There was no scenery. The entire play was performed against curtains on an improvised stage of about twenty feet square in the Grant Hall. Some 400 cadets were present. I never heard the play 'go' with such enthusiasm, understanding and responsiveness. At the conclusion every youngster threw his cap into the air with a shout and Irving made one of the happiest hits in his long series of speeches by declaring that 'the joy-bells are ringing in London tonight,' because for the first time in history the British have captured West Point!'[49]

There were times when the play went on without the benefit of Irving's acting; indeed, without the benefit of Irving's characterization. Norman Forbes, a member of Irving's company, often substituted for Irving when they were on tour. The notices varied considerably, but on the whole the critics were not unkind. Some felt that Forbes erred as they felt Irving had—in demanding more sympathy than the character deserved; while others thought that his Shylock was not the noble, unjustly persecuted character that Irving conceived. But the audiences were enthusiastic. It is difficult to appraise Forbes' performance. *The Post* called his interpretation "natural and rational," describing his Shylock as a "crabby, half-crazed fiend," implying that this was the normal, conventional interpretation.[50] Both *The Atheneum* and *The Times* disagreed with this view; *The Times* called Forbes "a mild Shylock, almost an apologetic Shylock,"[51] while *The Atheneum* wrote:

> . . . we wonder if the time is now forever fled when actors will see that a play such as this demands something more than prettiness and will give it the requisite infusion of passion.[52]

On this occasion, even the sets and the costumes were criticized. While they were considered in good taste, they were described as insipid and lacking in character. These were the same accessories that Irving used, but the master had become sacrosanct, and no

---

[48] March 19, 1888.

[49] Sir John Martin, *Autobiography,* London, 1933, p. 97.

[50] December 7, 1904.

[51] December 9, 1904.

[52] December 10, 1904.

critic had the temerity to be direct in criticizing any part of a production in which Irving himself appeared. The manifest dissatisfaction with the production that had been acclaimed in superlatives twenty-five years earlier brings us to the realization that its greatness had begun to pall. The world had changed, and in spite of the modifications, the production was out-of-date.

When Irving first presented *The Merchant of Venice* in 1879, the second-rate theatre was at its peak, and farces and comedies were the order of the day. The comic stage-Jew was still an effective source of revenue, but the laughter that he evoked at this time was not for the Jew, as such, according to Landa, but for the comic character he portrayed.[53] The distinction seems abstruse. Irving's production was accurately timed. But the world that surrounded the British stage had changed vastly in twenty-five years and the audience had changed with it. This new public was to witness the rebirth of thoughtful drama in the works of Ibsen, Pinero, Jones, Galsworthy and Shaw. Furthermore, during the twenty-five years of Irving's success, London Jewry had grown from 50,000 to 160,000, and by 1900 there were 270,000 Jews living in the British Isles. Mass violence and anti-Semitism in Russia were responsible for the flood of immigrants who were finding refuge in England, giving the business of selling cheap clothing, shoes, and furniture tremendous impetus. The Aliens Immigration Act in 1905 was framed to stem the tide of incoming East-European Jews.[54] The Jewish question was assuming larger proportions; it was the time of the Dreyfus affair. The Jews in England were no longer legally restricted but they lived in voluntary ghettos, apart from the world that continued to maintain a medieval prejudice against them. The Jewish question was about to become acute, and what had been inspiring in 1879 was no longer adequate in 1905.

Irving went on playing Shylock until the end of his life. During the period of his supremacy in the theatre, his fame mounted to monumental heights, but it did not entirely obscure the efforts of his less-gifted colleagues. At the same time that Irving was creating a theatre where the pleasure of the ear was matched by the pleasure of the eye, his fellow-actors were acquainting audiences with various other Shylocks. It is to them that we now turn our attention.

---

[53] Landa, *The Jew in Drama*, p. 218.
[54] Cecil Roth, *A Bird's-eye View of Jewish History*, Cincinnati, 1935, p. 355.

CHAPTER VI

Lesser Lights

IT is interesting to note that of all the Shakespearean plays presented on the London stage during the past fifty years, *The Merchant of Venice* is, after *Hamlet,* the most frequently produced. The roster of actors who have played Shylock during this period reads like a veritable "Who's Who in the Theatre." None of them built his reputation on Shylock as solidly as did Henry Irving. But the number of revivals, the length of the runs and the attention given to them by the press indicate the public's perennial interest in the play. Many actors leaned heavily on Irving's reading and borrowed freely from his production. But a few of them staked their careers on interpretations of Shylock that departed widely from Irving's venerated example. It may be of some interest to examine a number of these interpretations in the light of the Shylock tradition.

The Shylock of William Poel represents a thorough rejection of Irving's conception. In 1898, when Irving was at the zenith of his success with his aristocratic Shylock, Poel brought forth a red-wigged, middle-aged Jew of undeniably comic character. It was his intention to recapture with this creation his conception of the mood of Elizabethan England. Audiences found this Shylock extremely funny and Poel was encouraged to elaborate on his interpretation. In 1907, the Elizabethan Stage Society, of which he was founder and director, refined his production and fulfilled its *raison d'être* by presenting the play in strictly Elizabethan costumes on an Elizabethan stage. Act and scene divisions were eliminated; there were no pauses; the house lights were not dimmed. In spite of these gestures in the direction of authenticity, Poel's elaborated Shylock was not generally acclaimed by the critics. It was conceded that his venture

97

in Shakespearean staging was conscientious and important and he was praised for his thoroughgoing interpretation and his gay and light production, but the performance lacked depth.

This Shylock was meant to be mocked and scorned. The audience received him enthusiastically, but never took him seriously. His outbursts provoked the intended laughter, but the consequence was that he dragged the whole play down with him, and nobody cared much about Antonio either. The tragedy became a travesty; the comedy degenerated into slapstick. Some of the critics were offended by Poel's buffoonery, maintaining that this Shylock was a crazy pantaloon; not a man who was mad for revenge. Many contrasted him, inevitably, with Irving's Jew, whose character, they believed, accorded best with the spirit and the temper of the play.

Recent critics hold Poel's version in higher esteem than did his contemporaries, and his interpretation has acquired significance with time. In his study, *Shakespeare in the Theatre,* Poel argues that the spirit of comedy must be maintained throughout the play and that Shylock's tragic exit is out of place in a comic scene. According to him, Shylock should tear up the bond in great rage. He cites the suitability of the lines:

> Why, then the devil give him good of it!
> I'll stay no longer question.[1]

Unless the trial scene is played for its comedic values, Portia's doings in Act V are incongruous with the rest of the play.

Whatever may be said for this reasoning from the viewpoint of dramatic construction, it is evident that it would lead to the annihilation of one of Shakespeare's greatest characters. It would also effectively relegate *The Merchant of Venice* to the bookshelf. It may be that *The Merchant of Venice,* as we know it, is, to a certain extent, the creation of the actor, and that Shakespeare had no idea of writing a tragic part for Shylock, but those who feel this must assume not only the burden of the proof, but also the responsibility for the resulting interpretation.

*   *   *

With Herbert Beerbohm Tree, there was no question as to the tragic character of *The Merchant of Venice.* His Shylock was the serious, forceful character that Irving had created, though not quite

---

[1] London, 1913, p. 132.

as magnificent. Tree's wife, who incidentally preferred Irving's characterization, described her husband in the role as

> . . . passionate, long-suffering; by turns majestic and debased. . . . His large wistful eyes seemed to reveal the long tragic history of a persecuted race. . . . His perform-ance was undeviatingly picturesque . . . and compelling. It was religious.[2]

His appearance was that of a gentleman of fashion. He was des-cribed by Alexander Woollcott, in a later production, as willowy and almost effeminate, with "arms tossing like the fronds of a wind-swept tree."[3] But he was not the august and self-contained aristocrat depicted by his illustrious predecessor.

In Tree's characterization, the racial aspects of the pound of flesh story were emphasized as never before. Tree's prompt-book[4] calls for a set with the Jews living segregated on the far side of the canal, and the Jewish section was the last word in realistic staging, even to the Jewish wash hanging on the Jewish line. The attitude of these Jews, Tree advises, must always be servile. When Shylock is discovered, he is sitting among other residents of the ghetto. Tubal is in this scene; Shylock speaks the speech, "How like a fawning publican . . ." to him. He sits, making entries in a book, at the be-ginning of the "Signior Antonio" speech. When Antonio calls him "gentle Jew," he spits. In Act II, the Jews are seen going to the synagogue. "The harsh sounds of prayer are heard. Could there be a bell calling them to prayer?" Tree wonders. In one corner of the Jewish quarter, Shylock and his scales are seen at a window. Jessica is at an upper window, singing.

This Shylock is sincerely religious and practices the customs of his people. He is the traditionally good father and devoted widower. He leans affectionately on Jessica as they go to synagogue, but Jessica is soon able to slip away, since men and women sit separately at services. When Shylock leaves the synagogue, he bestows a kick upon Launcelot, who is asleep outside. A little later, Launcelot passes on this kick to a little Jewish boy who is also asleep. This is meant to be symbolic. Tree notes parenthetically and in some-

---

[2] Maud Tree, "Herbert and I," in *Herbert Beerbohm Tree,* collected by Max Beerbohm, London, (n.d.), p. 149.

[3] *World,* January 23, 1928.

[4] Folger Shakespeare Library.

what topsy-turvy order that "Jew kicks Christian, Christian kicks Jew, this is the story of the play." Accompanying Jessica, soon after, Gratiano and the others watch Shylock return to his empty house; they laugh as they exit. A quartet singing O *Sole Mio* serenaded the revellers in a later production in New York.

Tree's Shylock was an extremely dangerous character. His animosity was not particularly directed against Antonio; it turned against all persecutors of the Jews. In order to achieve this impression, Tree made Shylock intensely and even neurotically emotional. When Shylock returns home, to find Jessica and his money gone, he bursts into the house, rages through its rooms and appearing now at this window and now at that, cries out the name of his daughter in a crescendo, until he at last collapses. This bit of stage-business afforded Tree an excellent opportunity to impress his audience with his famous hoarse screeches, and he was generally admired for his ability to reproduce realistically the paroxysms of a man in great distress. Whenever Tree went into "fits", he never failed to delight his public. At the end, Shylock came dashing out of doors; he flung himself on the ground, and tore his garments. He sprinkled ashes on his head—all this to emphasize the "Jewish" quality of the Shylock scenes. But what a far cry from Irving's silent return![5]

Not only grief, but rage chokes Shylock in "no tear but of my shedding." Regardless of the expense, he tears his garments again; he beats the stones. In a moment he is down on his knees with "I thank God" as news of Antonio's plight reaches him. "I thank thee, good Tubal"––and he kisses his friend on both cheeks. He rushes to the synagogue at the end of the scene, "raising his arms to Jehovah to thank him for having smitten Antonio."[6]

It was, however, for his achievement in the trial scene that Tree was acclaimed as masterly. In this scene, he seemed to cast off his extravagance and to attain true Shakespearean heights. As the moment of revenge approached, his voice took on unusual clarity and resonance. He hammered out his words, one by one, punctuating them with the hilt of his knife against the table. His body was tense with malignant passion. His cunning, ferocity and sarcasm

---

[5] Granville-Barker later wrote that such lengthy elaboration of a distracted Shylock was inadmissible, since Shakespeare had deliberately avoided the situation. *Prefaces to Shakespeare,* p. 355, footnote.

[6] Tree's prompt-book, Folger Shakespeare Library.

were never so well brought out, but he weakened the scene by glancing continually at a little crowd of Jewish sympathizers on the stage, for approval and applause. So strongly was his adherence to the Jewish faith stressed, that his enforced conversion was seen to present a difficulty. Tree avoided the problem by making Shylock faint in Tubal's arms at the mention of conversion.

Although Tree was not imaginative, he was undoubtedly inventive. He was jibed at for thinking things up, rather than making them out. In the main, he was credited with an excellent "Venetian" production, against which he presented what was considered the most inspired of all his Shakespearean characterizations. That this best combined so many unsound elements is an indication of the level of public taste at the beginning of the twentieth century.

*   *   *

When Arthur Bourchier first played Shylock as an undergraduate at Oxford, the press considered the effort of the Philothespian Club sufficiently important to give it such coverage as professionals might envy. Bourchier resumed the role twenty years later, and he was hailed as remarkable. His acting version of *The Merchant of Venice* provided a clear and intelligible sequence. There were fourteen scene changes arranged into six acts,[7] but there were no liberties taken with Shakespeare's lines.

The sets were of special interest. They were praised for their realism, their simplicity and good taste. The scenery was easily shifted. The pauses were brief. One critic expressed gratification in the thought that the spectators could, at last, concentrate on the characters without being distracted by the over-elaborateness of detail. The simplicity of the production, although it gave promise of progress in the development of staging, was only relative. There were masques, street scenes, gondolas, and the usual singing and dancing, but on the whole, the production was characterized by speed, color, vigor and rich emotion.

The chief characteristic of this presentation was its tempo. The world itself, in 1905, was quickening its pace. The age of mechanization had dawned, and the program for the play at the Garrick Theatre carries an advertisement for a fifteen horse-power landaulette. But when Bourchier tried to keep up the pace in his acting,

---

[7] London, 1905.

he encountered some difficulty. As he started at what was considered top speed, he had no way of developing the scenes that required acceleration and heightened intensity. The traditional ponderous style of acting had not yet caught up with the technical advances of the time.

Bourchier's Shylock was a hard, practical, cold-blooded usurer, with nothing especially Jewish about him but his appearance. He looked imposing and picturesque in his curious Oriental shabbiness. There was a something of Judas in his face, but no suggestion of centuries of stored-up bitterness and suffering. This Shylock, nevertheless, had dignity, and Bourchier affected a general note of grandeur in the role. The part was played with quiet restraint. It was a clever and consistent conception that made no undue bid for audience sympathy and received none. Only when the Venetian revellers were brought back to the scene of Jessica's flight, in order to accentuate Shylock's tragedy, did Bourchier ask for an emotional response. It was not a romantic conception, and when Shylock left the courtroom, the audience felt that he had received the fate he deserved. There was no question of identification, or at least very little. One critic observed that we feel for Shylock the same sympathy we have for a wounded animal.

Bourchier stressed the differences between the Christians and the Jews in the play by labelling them as such and by listing them separately on the program. Little by little he simplified the production. By 1907, when he presented the play in the Stratford Festival, much of the spectacle was omitted. There remained the portrayal of the revengeful money-lender, in a straightforward piece of skilful acting, without complexity and without subtlety. Several years later, in a lecture at Oxford, Bourchier analyzed the character of Shylock as one made evil by persecution. Recalling the recent massacres of Jews in Russia, he pointed out the dangers to humanity when a minority is treated brutally. The analysis was, doubtless, valuable, but the characterization left a good deal to the imagination.

*   *   *

Richard Mansfield won fame in the role of Shylock on both sides of the Atlantic and over a long period of years, but his contribution appears to have been largely cosmetic. His make-up was spectacular, and he was praised more for his long grey beard than for his harsh and unsympathetic portrayal. Nevertheless, his purpose, at the outset, was to emphasize every redeeming human quality he could find in the money-lender and to win active sympathy for the despised and persecuted figure.

But as Mansfield developed the character over the years, he consistently changed his interpretation until Shylock finally became repulsive. Little by little, the injured Jew lost his sensibilities and became the embodiment of implacable hatred. A lifetime of revilement had made him evil. Mansfield may not have realized how strongly he stressed Shylock's malevolence. He wrote in a letter to William Winter:

> Damn your criticisms! . . . I had a deuce of a time getting
> our only patrons, the Jews, to come and see *The Merchant,*
> because *you* made me out a fiend and a vulture.[8]

Mansfield read Shylock's lines with a slight accent, broadening the short *i* into "preenciple" and "Chreestian." He spat when he addressed Antonio, but he embraced Jessica tenderly and he kissed her on the forehead. He gave a "yell of surprise and agony" when he found that his daughter had fled and he rushed furiously into the street amid "the hoots of the delighted Christians."[9]

His lust for revenge was evident throughout the trial scene. He sprang madly at Antonio to plunge his knife into the merchant's breast. He knew every word of the bond by heart and though he clutched it in his trembling hand, he did not have to glance at it when he told Portia, "I cannot find it." The young judge was an enigma to him and his gaze never faltered as it pierced Portia's eyes. He continued with a slow, heavy and resentful tone, "'tis not in the bond." When he was offered thrice the sum of the loan, his friends inspected the ducats and pleaded with him to accept it. Shylock paused grimly, then dashed the gold upon the ground.[10] By the time he was ready to make his last exit, he had turned the knife upon himself and his last speech was scarcely audible.[11]

[8] *Theatre Magazine,* June, 1910, p. 195.

[9] Arthur Colby Sprague, *Shakespeare And The Actors,* Cambridge, 1945, p. 23.

[10] William Winter, *Shakespeare On The Stage,* First Series, New York, 1911, p. 193.

[11] *Ibid.,* p. 199.

It is interesting to note that the first time that Edison's incandescent light was used in a theatre it was in Mansfield's *The Merchant of Venice*. It is to be hoped that the inventor illuminated the play better than did the actor.

*   *   *

E. H. Sothern considered his Shylock one of his best roles, but a study of his treatment of *The Merchant of Venice* leaves us doubtful as to the wisdom of his judgment. He was esteemed as one of the foremost actors of his day and he had an enthusiastic following. Neither Charles Frohman, who presented him, nor Lee Shubert, who directed the production in the early 1900's, can be accused of stinginess. It seems to have been lavish in everything but intelligence and good taste.

The play opened with an operatic overture on a street scene crowded with singers, mandolin players, a fortune teller, a flower seller and two fruit stands. Then Shylock entered with Tubal and another Jew. He had two heavy curls for a beard and his face was made up to resemble Michelangelo's Moses. His costume was severely black and did not suggest wealth. He wore earrings but no hat. In Sothern's version, the idea of Antonio's forfeit came to Shylock as a spontaneous impulse; a mere jest. Later in the scene, as soon as Jessica caught a glimpse of her father, she sprang with Launcelot into a gondola.

In Act II of this production, Jessica is found stroking her father's hand; she helps him on with his coat. Further along in the scene, when Shylock crosses the bridge on his way home, his cane pushes aside a scarf and a mask left by the revellers. Act III opens, immediately after Jessica's flight, with Shylock, Salanio, and Salarino on the stage. This scene, too, is crowded with un-Shakespearean "business." Women and children trail after Shylock; a boy has hold of his cloak. Shylock strikes at him with his cane; the boy dodges. Another boy gets Shylock's cap and throws it about. Now the Portia scenes come. During the trial scene in Act IV, the flock of supernumeraries of Act I are pressed into service again as peasants, pages and soldiers. Shylock, who is particularly active in the court-room, playing a veritable dumb-show, kneels and kisses the hem of Julia Marlowe's gown on "A Daniel come to judgment!" He crushes the bond in his hand. When Portia insists, "Thou shalt have nothing but the forfeiture," he picks up the knife in rage and starts toward Antonio, only to throw it down in impotent fury. With the scales dangling from his belt, he snatches the bond from Portia and tears it into fragments. When told by Portia to tarry and beg for mercy, he promptly faints, and when Gratiano offers to assist him, he pushes him away. On Antonio's suggestion that he turn Christian, he cries out like a hunted beast, protesting "with both hands." In animal fashion, he tries to escape from the room. The guard stops him. Then he stretches out a hand in supplication toward the Duke. Tubal and another Jew turn from Shylock, pulling their garments from his grasp, and at last, Shylock staggers toward a soldier and falls upon his spear. But he has not yet finished. With a derisive sound and a look of withering scorn at Gratiano, he walks out erect, breaks down, falls, almost, "doubled up, with his hands on his head." The "other" Jew offers to follow him, but is restrained by Tubal. It is clear that Sothern saw the play neither as tragic nor as comic. It was pure melodrama.

*   *   *

When Robert B. Mantell was presented in *The Merchant of Venice* in World War I days, it was in a production that utilized the prompt-book made for Edwin Booth by William Winter. He appeared in Puritan costume, with an unkempt beard and his head uncovered. It is not easy to evaluate his work, since, for the most part, the press ignored Mantell's delineation of Shylock. Only one unsound change was singled out for consideration. In Act I, Scene 3, Mantell ended the scene abruptly on Antonio's speech:

> Content, i' faith, I'll seal to such a bond,
> And say there is much kindness in the Jew.

With this Antonio and Bassanio exit. Shylock is left alone. He inhales once deeply, deliberately strides forward, extends his right hand, which seems suddenly to have become palsied, and as he viciously draws his fingers together in a clutching gesture, the curtain falls. There were both hisses and applause. The success of this *coup de theatre* occasioned some debate, but it can hardly be considered a contribution to the development of the character.

*   *   *

Best known for bringing *Cyrano de Bergerac* before American audiences, Walter Hampden extended his repertory in the early twenties to include *The Merchant of Venice*. Several critics considered Shylock his best role. Robert Garland thought it the most vivid portrayal of the Jew he had ever seen and commended Hampden for the hard, brittle and unflaggingly vindictive quality he gave to Shylock,[12] but a number of playgoers described his interpretation as one that appealed most to anti-Semites. Indeed, Hampden, by deleting the first scene in Portia's home, and replacing it with the scene in which Launcelot contemplates leaving the employ of Shylock, began by presenting the Jew in a most unfriendly light before he even made his entrance. The rest of the characterization was quite consistent with this aim.

In outward appearance, Hampden's Shylock was a traditional ghetto Jew with a fringed shawl over his robe and straggly earlocks that framed a bitter, bitten face. What Hampden was trying to develop was the keen, unbending and stern character of an arch-fiend, but his guttural enunciation, his habit of pawing the scenery and spitting on the other characters made of this Shylock a veritable animal. The character was not taken seriously. *The Weekly Review* called it squalid, aged, unbalanced and hysterical, and reminded its readers that the text did not require Shylock to be all or any of these things.[13] Most damaging was the opinion that Hampden failed to enlist the concern of the audience for Shylock.

*   *   *

Long before Maurice Moskovitch undertook Shylock as his first English-speaking role, he was known in London's East End for having played the part in Yiddish and in Russian in a version with which he had toured the globe. His familiarity with the character was recognized at once in his English presentation and he was lauded by the London critics for his competent acting. It was his theatrical skill and not his interpretation of Shylock that brought him approval. Landa describes the disillusionment of his Yiddish-speaking audiences, in his early acting days,[14] when they could discover nothing extraordinary in Shakespeare's play. To them, it was the worst form of travesty. What they attributed to Shakespeare was, in reality, the mockery of Moskovitch's characterization, and

---

[12] *Baltimore American,* November 15, 1922.

[13] O. W. Firkus, May 28, 1921.

[14] M. J. Landa, *The Shylock Myth,* London, 1942, p. 37f.

it was this that he carried over to the English stage. His sensational success saw him through an initial run of more than two hundred performances during the 1919-20 season and his Shylock became the talk of London. Ten years later, it made news in New York.

In a realistic and elaborately staged three-act production, Moskovitch appeared, a six foot, one inch Shylock, whose make-up was praised as being the most repulsive that had ever been seen. He resembled a fat, crazed, unpleasant spider. So convincing was his acting that his Shylock, "greasy, snuffling," with "not a shred of dignity" was considered by one critic to be an authentic replica of Shakespeare's Jew. Moskovitch was a realist, and this Shylock was neither a prophet nor a public monument; he was an ordinary, every-day huckster, imbued with a spirit of revenge. Moskovitch so played up the malignant character of Shylock that many spectators felt that while they did not condone, they began to understand pogroms. One critic could only sputter, "overwhelmingly alive and grotesquely deadly, an obsession, a nightmare. Ugh!" The critic on *The Post*, however, did not feel that this Shylock was particularly dangerous. He described him as a "smiling, chuckling, well-nourished, ill-conditioned, and evil-disposed elderly usurer of no great distinction, who seems more amused than anything else when chance brings Antonio into his clutches."[15]

Moskovitch's Shylock fairly jumped for joy when he heard from Tubal the news of Antonio's misfortune. Concern for money was such an integral part of his character that it was natural for him to confuse the loss of his daughter with the loss of his jewels and his ducats. In the trial scene, he carefully removed his rings so as not to soil them with his victim's blood. He seized Antonio and forced him to his knees, adding non-Shakespearean imprecations in Yiddish. His extravagant gestures and mannerisms turned the trial scene into slapstick, and while several critics felt that he had sold Shylock's tragedy for a laugh, others believed that he had taken undue advantage of the few famous lines in order to transform Shylock suddenly into a martyr. When his plot was foiled, he made faces at the court in impotent rage, his body writhing. The last impression left by Moskovitch when he quit the stage was that he had robbed the moment of its last touch of pathos. It was

---

[15] November 4, 1919.

not until later, when he played the stellar role in Ashley Duke's adaptation of Feuchtwanger's *Jew Süss*, that he convinced his public that he could sustain a role with dignity.

*   *   *

Rarely has a play been heralded with more fanfare than the production of *The Merchant of Venice* that starred David Warfield as Shylock. It was lavishly staged during the 1922-23 season by David Belasco, but New York audiences gazed at the splendor of the sumptuous presentation, and were unimpressed. Had Belasco limited his "improvements" only to the architectural details of his sets, these would have won for him new laurels in the field of realistic staging. But with a microscopic eye for *minutiae* and a mania for piling on properties, he completely missed the essence of the play.

A special edition of *The Merchant of Venice,* based on the Belasco production,[16] reveals a script that is little short of ludicrous. Shakespeare's text is wantonly slashed; scenes are interpolated; lines are transplanted and invented. The text of this mangled version is in the direct line of descent from Granville's, although the changes are, in spirit at least, quite remote from the eighteenth century adaptation. No other modern Shakespearean production had suffered such textual maltreatment. Act III, in this rearrangement, is an accumulation of the Portia-in-Belmont scenes, and keeps Shylock offstage for almost an hour. Three months' action is condensed into one act. A cantor introduces Shylock's first scene, intoning prayers in Hebrew, with the assistance of a choir. The Rialto is situated in the ghetto, with a synagogue center-stage. People are on their way to a service; some are in prayer shawls. Through the open door of the synagogue, the congregation can be seen, and against this background Antonio and Shylock discuss the terms of the bond. The atmosphere suggests that created by Beerbohm Tree, but Tree's regard for Shakespeare was positively reverent in comparison.

Warfield's Shylock had a slight, drooping figure, emaciated hands, a scrawny beard and a long pinched nose. As an individual with a deep family tragedy as well as an incidental eye for business, he was pathetic, but he lacked dignity. Signing the bond was a

---

[16] New York, 1922.

casual thing for him—an every-day banking matter. There was no cunning involved here. Shylock was merely trying to buy friendship by making a gratuitous loan. One critic found him vivid, convincing, illuminating. "He makes you pity the poor, hectored money-lender even as you despise his pettiness."[17] He was an insignificant but comprehensible human being, and audiences were able to understand his familiar Jewish gestures. It was only later, by repeated and undeserved provocations, that he was stung to madness and revenge. But even when he had reached his peak of emotion, he was completely overshadowed by the huge canvas. It was as if Belasco were trying constantly to demonstrate the insignificance of any human tragedy in the vastness of the universe. When last seen, Shylock is restrained by Gratiano, while a monk raises a crucifix before him. The on-lookers in the courtrom jeered and hooted as he made his exit but apparently the on-lookers in the audience did not share either joy or sorrow.

A financially profitable nation-wide tour, following the New York run, served only to demonstrate to the rest of the country how blasting a disappointment this production was. Warfield's reputation, however, was not seriously impaired. He continued to be lovingly remembered as the Music Master and as Peter Grimm.

*　　*　　*

The most regal of all Shylocks was George Arliss. He brought a certain majesty to all his characters, and this patrician tone was evident in his Shylock, as well. In an impressive, skilfully-cut version of *The Merchant of Venice* which Winthrop Ames presented in 1928, Arliss played a suave, rich, well-tailored Oriental Jew. In the early part of the play, to demonstrate Shylock's contempt of the Christians, he allowed himself an occasional chuckle. Beyond this he made no concessions to comedy. Something of the primness and severity of this treatment may be ascribed to Arliss' own Jewish origin. Arliss may have felt the necessity of re-establishing Shylock's dignity, after the damaging effects of Moskovitch's interpretation of the Jew. At any rate, he presented the only characterization he knew how to create—that of an austere and discreet gentleman, and whatever his reason may have been, the atmosphere of Jewish tradition was conspicuously absent from his performance.

---

[17] *Los Angeles Express,* March 9, 1924.

There was nothing particularly pathetic about this Shylock. He was a stoic, and had no use for what George M. Cohan used to call "the gravy." This Shylock refused to admit to the world or to himself that he was at all distraught at the disappearance of his daughter and his ducats. He knocked twice on the locked door. Later, he returned to the deserted house. He started to knock once more, but remembering the futility of doing that, he drew away his hand. That was all.

On the other hand, he was a master-mind, like Disraeli. From the beginning to the very end of the play, he plotted insidiously, almost playfully, with sardonic malice. His crafty and indomitable ways were no less sinister because they were ingratiating. In the trial scene, he continued to be the cultured and well-mannered broker. It was the general opinion of those who saw Arliss in the role that this was an intelligent analysis of the part. But if he kept his poise and lost his climax, it was because the interpretation was too cerebral. It was merely a dignified British gentleman who happened to be playing Shylock.

*   *   *

The Merchant of Venice has long been a favorite in the Old Vic repertory, but for many years its treatment of the play was conventional. While it made a number of innovations, these were largely in the spirit of overshadowing other productions by the inclusion of new bits of stage business. Matheson Lang played Shylock in a 1914 presentation, where the only new handling of the play was to be found in the staging of the Shylock scenes. These were taken from the public square and placed inside Shylock's house so that Jessica could be seen flitting about and the effect of her flight upon her father could be emphasized.

When John Gielgud began his career as a producer by presenting *The Merchant of Venice* for the Old Vic in 1932, he made no attempt to equate the casket and the pound of flesh plots. Rather, they were sharply contrasted so that their marked dissimilarities might be pointed up. Many years before, an attempt had been made to shift the emphasis from the Shylock role. Charles F. Coghlan, in Bancroft's production of the play in 1875, had conceived Shylock as a man of indistinct character. He was irresolute and weak. He neither stirred nor impressed his audience, but left them, rather, apathetic to Shylock. The reason for this treatment was to throw into relief the character of Portia, who was, for the first time, the center of the play. But this was because Ellen Terry was assuming the role. Odell disagrees with the opinion that Coghlan had intentionally created a vague Shylock. He dubs the performance a pitiable failure, while, at the same time, calling Coghlan a superb actor when cast in an appropriate role, citing his success in the *School for Scandal* revival.[18] In Gielgud's production, the Portia story was presented as a fantasy, while the Shylock tale was treated realistically.

The critics were particularly impressed with this "fairy tale" quality of Gielgud's presentation. Granville-Barker recognizes the reality of Shylock's personality in this treatment, but the remainder of the story, in his opinion, remains fabulous. The bond plot, as well as the will of Portia's father, is a fantasy, and is about as credible as *Jack and the Beanstalk*. This, however, does not weaken Shylock's actuality.[19] By cutting any part of the play, the swift antiphony of the Shylock and Portia stories is destroyed.[20] As early as 1920, the play had been given such a mythical interpretation, when, in the only Old Vic Shakespearean production of the season to receive any attention from the press, the casket plot was given more than its usual emphasis, while Shylock was made less the center of interest. Several years later, when Baliol Holloway was presented with the Old Vic company, he played Shylock as a wholly evil person, who was kept in the background. The entire bond plot was subordinated to the mood of poetry and imagination of the fairy tale. No one had any need to worry about Shylock here. He was only the witch in the fairy tale.

This treatment of the play provided the basis for Gielgud's interpretation, and his production was designed to further his intention. The settings were created by Gielgud and were highly praised. Only a few critics accused him of "fantasticating too much,"[21] and of overloading it with too much dancing, music and elaborate decoration. The costumes were not designed for historical accuracy.

---

[18] Odell, *Shakespeare from Betterton to Irving*, vol. II, pp. 261-62.

[19] *Prefaces to Shakespeare*, pp. 335, 353.

[20] *Associating with Shakespeare*, London, 1932, p. 11.

[21] John Gielgud, *Easy Stages*, New York, 1939, p. 214.

They were related only to the characters they clothed and to the general scheme of color and design. Shylock's costume looked impressively expensive, but it was made of dish-cloths. Malcolm Keen played Shylock in a realistic and powerful key, but he was not allowed to dominate the action of the play. The entire production was musically and pictorially rich; frankly picturesque and unrealistic. The most serious flaw in this version was its obvious lack of unity. *The Spectator* compared it to a meal "served as a series of courses as distinct as a sausage, a chop, a rasher, and a kidney."[22]

Gielgud persisted in this interpretation. In 1938, he himself appeared as Shylock and gave further evidence of his intention to keep the play from becoming the tragedy of the Jew. At no time did he sentimentalize the role. He was a somewhat common and young-looking Shylock, almost bald, with curled earlocks and a straggly beard, who "skillfully combined squalid ignobility with fine dignity."[23] Only a few of the critics objected to the playing of Shylock as a nuisance instead of a menace. In spite of Gielgud's efforts, the critics remained stubbornly aware of Shylock. Gielgud contended that the trial scene provided the drama; Shylock's knife, the melodrama. It was precisely this aspect that interested the critics. Gielgud attempted to play down Shylock, but he was remembered best for his loquacious hands and for his "gummy, blinking eyes, that suggested some nasty creature in the dark."[24] Whatever Gielgud's intention may have been, *The Merchant of Venice* continued to be a Shylock play for the critic who wrote:

> Never have his [Gielgud's] remarkable gifts been shown to greater advantage, and when he is on the stage you can feel the whole house motionless under the painful weight of his realism.[25]

Far from providing a standardized characterization, a more recent Old Vic production, directed by Michael Benthall, presented Robert Helpmann, the accomplished dancer, whose movements as Shylock were described by one critic as "a miracle of grace." His interpreta-

---

[22] December 16, 1932.

[23] *Post,* April 22, 1938.

[24] *New Statesman and Nation,* May 7, 1938.

[25] *Ibid.*

tion, however, missed the greatness and grandeur of the man.[26] This correspondent saw Shylock as

> . . . a brave man. He faced up to the baitings of the Venetian hobbledehoys, and he had pride of race, and was never the humble, servile Jew, even to serve his own ends. He hated Antonio, with double reason, for the Merchant was a rival in trade and also a Jew baiter. Shylock should loom over the play like a dark cloud of vengeance, wanting that pound of flesh. . . . At the end, when he is tricked so shamefully by Portia, he should display a dignity which arouses sympathy and pity. Mr. Helpmann does not succeed in giving us all of this. There are some flashes of it but not enough to make this a notable Shylock or even a first rank one.

Another recent British Shylock who disappointed the critics was Emlyn Williams, who presented a repellent-looking Jew in dirty clothes and matted hair in a Stratford-on-Avon production. In a performance that failed to stir the heart enough to suggest the Jew's dignity and stature, Williams seemed more concerned with making melodramatic effects than with expressing feelings.

On this side of the Atlantic most Shylock actors have fared no better. John Carradine's Jew was subdued and reserved.[27] Luther Adler, in a New York City Center production, gave the effect "that he is the helpless and uncomprehending victim of a system to which he is indispensable financially but intolerable socially."[28] Clarence Derwent was described by Brooks Atkinson as "a rather amiable though resentful old codger who does not have much vitality left."[29]

Providing summer theatre-goers and lovers of Shakespeare with the opportunity to renew their interest in the bard has been the establishment of two community theatres—one in Stratford, Ontario, and the other in Stratford, Connecticut. Included in the Canadian repertory in 1955 was Tyrone Guthrie's production of *The Merchant of Venice* with Frederick Valk, the late Czech actor, as a good-natured, if cautious Shylock. His easy-going acceptance of the

---

[26] *Morning Telegraph*, New York, January 3, 1957.

[27] *Los Angeles Times*, December 8, 1943.

[28] *New Yorker*, March 14, 1953.

[29] *New York Times*, January 8, 1958.

pound of flesh forfeit changed only after he discovered his daughter's stealth. Critics and audience concurred in their admiration of the tension that Valk created in the trial scene in his splendid interpretation of the badgering of a strong man of dignity.

In the Stratford, Connecticut 1957 production, Morris Carnovsky's Shylock was also marked by dignity. Walter Kerr commended him for not begging for sympathy, terming him a superb Shylock[30] . . . "a rigid titan as he stalks up . . . into the court." He was somewhat less generous of the "Hath not a Jew eyes" speech, spotlighted like an operatic aria and spoken like "a quote from the play instead of a cutting episode in it." Other critics praised Carnovsky for his depth of perception and for the vigor and humor that he brought to the part. Henry Hewes described how this Shylock, in the midst of his grief, hearing that Antonio's ships have been lost

> . . . breaks into a magnificently ludicrous dance of glee. Even in the courtroom he gets a fine laugh, when he berates the men for offering to sacrifice their wives with "These be Christian husbands." This humor only makes the characterization more complete, and when Shylock finally leaves, sick at heart, he is an unforgettable picture of a human made small by his own smallness.[31]

There have been a number of other famous Shylocks in the earlier days of the modern theatre—Forbes-Robertson, Ben Greet, and Otis Skinner outstanding among them. If we mention their names only in passing, it is because their interpretations, while technically skillful and dramatically convincing, followed in the footsteps of their predecessors and failed to shed new light on the character of Shylock.

---

[30] *New York Herald Tribune,* July 11, 1957.

[31] *Saturday Review,* July 27, 1955.

CHAPTER VII

Shylock Distorted

THE HISTORY of Shylock on the stage would be incomplete without an account of how he fared in the second-rate theatre. The bond plot, because of the nature of the situation that it dramatizes, has always been a most fertile field for experimentation. Granville's *The Jew of Venice* is illustrative of such effort in the realm of sensationalism. The treatment that Shakespeare's play has received at the hands of more recent adapters stands as further illustration of the uncreative borrowing from Shakespearean sources. Since the beginning of the nineteenth century, dramatic ventures that do not seem to have been deserving of production were undertaken with enthusiasm. For every farce, melodrama, comic-opera, dramatic reading, and recitation that was printed and published after having been successfully presented on the stage, there were, of course, dozens that were produced but never printed. When the music-halls came into existence, many of the "legitimate" theatres were relieved of the burden of carrying these dramatic vehicles. At the same time, the theatres lost the patronage of those who had flocked thither mainly to see the novelties.

In the years during which vaudeville was popular, the trial scene of *The Merchant of Venice* competed gallantly with trained-dog acts and acrobatic displays. It was necessary, under such circumstances, for the actor to emphasize the melodramatic aspects of Shakespeare's scene, in order to make it self-sustaining, and some of our best actors, over a period of decades, lent themselves to this practice. They appeared in drastically "cut" versions of the scene during "off-seasons" in order to supplement their incomes and to remain in the limelight. Some versions, of course, presented

115

Shylock in his worst possible aspect. He was not a man with freedom to come and go and to transact business; he was not an individual who spoke up against the injustices that he had experienced; nor a father and a husband who had lost what once was his. Shakespeare had made him all of these, but the precisely-timed "skit" found him useful chiefly as a fiend with a knife in his hand.

Shylock was not the only stage-Jew in the theatre at this time. The line of Jewish dramatic characters in the eighteenth century had grown extensive. The descendants of the "Ol'-Clo's" men had taken on a certain stature. They still gesticulated wildly and comically; their speech was an unmistakable sing-song, but they were beginning to show more likable traits. In Montague Glass' dramatizations, Abe Potash and Mawruss Perlmutter made friends among the gentiles, and their popularity lasted well into the twentieth century. If their derby hats were several sizes too large, if they were petty in their bickering, only the Jews in the audience, sensitized by generations of dramatic plaguing, were embarrassed.

Besides, it was now Jews who were writing about Jews. For the gentile world, this was all good-natured fun. They had known these Jews for a long time and somehow their social offenses seemed merely amusing. Their idiosyncrasies were conspicuous, but no more so than those that were portrayed by the stage-Irishman or the stage-Dutchman. In the 1920's, with Ann Nichols' *Abie's Irish Rose,* the Jew and the Irishman were equated socially and were playfully satirized. From this time on, in America, at least, the Jew ceased to be a caricature on the stage. The delineations of Jewish characters in such plays as Elmer Rice's *Counsellor-at-Law,* Clifford Odets' *Awake and Sing,* Maxwell Anderson's *Winterset,* Franz Werfel's *Jacobovsky and the Colonel,* and Arthur Laurents' *Home of the Brave* are sufficiently fresh in our memories to obviate the necessity for discussion. Anti-Semitism continues to find expression in many phases of twentieth century life; in the drama, at least for the time, it has disappeared.

Prior to this period, while the characterization that met with the greatest approval was the one that was thought to be consonant with the late nineteenth century liberal viewpoints, many conventionalized portrayals of the Jew continued to exist on the stage. But whether he was a dignified Jewish gentleman who had been wronged, or a repulsive monster who sought revenge, Shylock remained a familiar figure. Each generation found theatre-goers who knew at least a dozen actors' portrayals of Shakespeare's Jew. In the second-rate theatre he was no less popular, but he had a special function there. Once Shylock made his bow, he remained as the uncontested protagonist of a number of plays that were written only for the purpose of making him appear ridiculous.

Among these is *Shylock: or the Merchant of Venice Preserved*. Francis N. Talfourd's burlesque is remembered on two scores. Not only was it deemed worthy of publication, but in the Shylock of Frederick Robson it found a characterization that was to last many years. It was printed as "an entirely new reading of Shakespeare, from an edition hereto undiscovered by modern authorities, and which it is hoped will be received as the stray leaves of a Jerusalem hearty-joke."[1] The painful pun must have delighted its maker, for playbills soon appeared, sub-sub-titling the piece *A Jerusalem Hearty Joke.*

Robson was a tragedian of considerable reputation when he first lent his talents to this novelty. He had been pronounced by some of the best critics as the greatest actor on the London stage since Edmund Kean. This was far from niggardly praise, and there was no indication that he ever regretted his change in category. When the Talfourd "extravaganza," as it was often billed, was first produced at the Royal Olympic Theatre in 1853, Shylock was featured as "a Jew who does not on this occasion conduct himself as a Gentile-man." As may be suspected, the plot clung with suffocating closeness to Shakespeare's, and at a period when *The Merchant of Venice* was enjoying a peak of popularity in the sober portrayals of Charles Kean and his contemporaries, its farcical counterpart nourished itself on the energy and the prestige of their productions. It was usually preceded by another farce, as if to assure for it, in advance, the laughing approval that it invariably received. It swaggered through a number of revivals in England and America, and as late as 1868, when Booth's tragic treatment of Shylock was most highly acclaimed, it continued to be hailed as a novelty.

The laughter did not subside with Talfourd's play. It spread, in fact, like contagion, and the theatre became infected with a

---

[1] London, 185?.

rash of Shylock burlesques. A travesty on the trial scene, with the inexcusable title, *The Peddler of Very Nice*[2] has Shylock as a pawn-broker, Antonio as a peddler and Portia as "a Very Nice bloomer girl." But like the fashion it ridiculed, the one-act play was not long-lived.

More enduring was John Brougham's *Much Ado About A Merchant of Venice*.[3] Brougham was a competent comedian who had written a number of burlesques based on classical and historical characters that were regarded by several reputable drama critics as intelligent, if not intellectual, works. He encountered great success in America with his sportive version of Shakespeare's comedy, which was described as being "from the original text—a long way." The play consisted largely of a series of barbs thrown at some of the well-known Wall Street financiers and their operations. From the time of its first presentation in 1868, Brougham's piece was regarded as altogether delightful and almost until the close of the century, when its topical references had lost most of their significance, it continued to be a favorite. Brander Matthews spoke of Brougham, who excelled in Irish roles, as "an amusing, but rather Hibernian Shylock."[4] An interleafing in a prompter's copy of the play notes that "Shylock is a painfully ill-used, and persecuted old Hebrew gentleman—in fact, an Israelite of other days, whose character was darkened by his Christian contemporaries simply to conceal their own nefarious transactions; victimized as he was by sundry unjustifiable confidence operations."

A cartoon advertising Brougham's burlesque exhibits the familiar three-ball symbol of the pawnshop in the background and a droll Shylock, beset by various misfortunes, not the least of which are a pair of Charlie Chaplin feet, a sour countenance and a hook nose. "My deeds upon my head" is taken quite literally by the artist; weighing down that tragically comic figure is a heap of documents, labelled Bonds and Deeds.[5] In spite of the broadness of this caricature, Brougham's Shylock was enthusiastically received and it proved that an exploited Shylock could be as ridiculous as a villainous one.

[2] By George Melville Baker, Boston, 1866.
[3] New York, 1868.
[4] *Playwrights on Playmaking*, New York, 1923, p. 286.
[5] Theatre Collection, Houghton Library, Harvard University.

Other plays of this period that do not, on reading, seem to be worth the paper on which they were printed but that somehow found their way to the stage, are "a burlesque extravaganza" called *The Merry Merchant of Venice,* coyly sub-titled, *A Peep at Shakespeare Through the Venetians,*[6] which finds Shylock "in the pawn-broking and old clo' line," and *Petruchio's Widow,*[7] a one-act travesty whose chief characters are Mr. Moses Shylock, a pawn-broker, and Mrs. Jessica Lorenzo, an ungrateful daughter. Although we derive some brief satisfaction from the knowledge that such plays did not enjoy lasting favor, their inclusion among the farces of the day indicates how low Shylock could be brought. Further vulgarization of Shakespeare's character is to be found in *The Shakespeare Water-Cure,*[8] a burlesque in three acts, where Shylock, described as "crafty and greedy," is involved in plotting to acquire Portia's fortune. This character reaches the height of cunning by bribing Lady Macbeth to incite her husband to murder Bassanio so that he can be free to marry the heiress.

Equally distasteful is *The (Old Clothes) Merchant of Venice: or The Young Judge and Old Jewry,*[9] by a discreetly anonymous author. Another squib of this type, demurely entitled *The Merchant of Venice,*[10] is "only slightly revised and modernized" but can be readily distinguished from the original. It is a foolish burlesque that attempts to suit the incidents of the Shakespeare play to the contingencies of a football team and it was sufficiently popular in its time to survive two printed editions. More recently, *Shakespeare in Wall Street*[11] was dignified with publication by one of the most reputable publishing houses. Nonsensically described "a burlesque in the form of a Shakespearean tragedy," the scene is laid in New York and New Jersey at the time of a stock market crash. Among its characters are Shakespeare, Mrs. Shakespeare, Shylock and a modern stock broker. There have undoubtedly been other Shylock burlesques, but these will suffice to demonstrate the tradition.

---

[6] Frederick John Fraser, Allahabad, 1895.

[7] George Morely Vickers, Philadelphia, 1888.

[8] The Larks (pseudo.), New York, 1883.

[9] New York, 1884.

[10] Carl S. Miner (and others), Cedar Rapids, 1896 (?).

[11] Edward H. Warren, Houghton Mifflin Co., Boston, 1929.

Not all of the "Shylock plays" were comic or trivial. A number of writers whose motives for dealing with Shakespeare's Jew were far from funny, saw a serious literary challenge in visualizing a Venice that went beyond the courtroom. Some of them dealt with the effects on Shylock of the sentence that was imposed on him; others. mused over the quality of Portia's mercy that would permit her, in later years, to live with the knowledge that she had duped the money-lender by a clever trick. There were sober and thoughtful considerations of the former in Ludwig Lewisohn's novel, *The Last Days of Shylock*[12] and in a translation from the Hebrew of Ibn-Sahav's *Jessica, My Daughter,*[13] which saw gratifying production in a Yiddish dramatization by Maurice Schwartz, but these cannot be discussed within the limits of this study.

In *A Dramatic Reverie,*[14] a serious dramatic undertaking produced at Sadler's Wells in 1856, Shylock was seen as the victim of injustice. The play is written in competent blank verse; its author, Richard Hengist Horne, appeared as Shylock in his own version of the trial scene. He had based his dramatization on an article called *Shylock: A Critical Fancy,*[15] which had appeared almost two decades before, and he made it clear that he intended not to substitute his work for Act IV of Shakespeare's play, but to offer it as a speculation of what might have passed through Shylock's mind, had the trial been held in Venice in 1850. The thoughtful writer has supplied the details of what Shylock might have said, had he been better versed in physiology, to meet the quibble regarding the taking of flesh without shedding blood. The scene opens as Shakespeare wrote it and proceeds with the original lines until Portia's "Tarry a little" speech. Shylock then insists on his bond, stating his willingness to take the pound of flesh, little by little, by installments. Portia finds him guilty of plotting to take the life of a Venetian citizen. The Duke calls him "a bearded vulture." His punishment is the same as that meted out to him in Shakespeare's play, but he exits from the courtroom in a wild state of fury.

---

[12] New York, 1931.

[13] New York, 1948.

[14] Reprinted in Furness' Variorum *The Merchant of Venice,* p. 400ff.

[15] *Ibid.*

Among the serious experiments with the story must be numbered *The Third Age*,[16] which presents a strange and contrary outcome to the trial scene, and *The Merchant of Venice, Act VI*,[17] which finds Shylock, following the trial, despised by the Christians, accepting conversion and publicly professing his adherence to Christianity. He remains a Jew at heart, true to his faith and secretly nursing his passion for revenge. A more diffused treatment of the theme is to be found in *A New Shylock*, which was first produced at London's Lyric Theatre in 1914, with Louis Calvert as the Jew. In this play, the daughter of a money-lender runs away with a Christian who, in the end, becomes a Jew. Here there is greater departure from Shakespeare's plot than in the other adaptations. To complicate the story further, the money-lender who had hoped that his son would be a rabbi, sorrows to see that he has turned, instead, into a shady businessman.

Shylock Returns[18] dramatizes Shylock in his later years, relating in two scenes, the fates of those who were involved in Shakespeare's play. Ten years after the trial scene, Antonio is dead and Jessica returns to her father. This variant of the Prodigal Son theme was first presented in Sydney, Australia. *The Quality of Mercy*,[19] another sixth-act treatment, takes the form of a revery, following the reading of Shakespeare's play. It saw production in San Francisco in 1928, the same year that *A Pound of Flesh*[20] was being presented in Hollywood. This last is a one-act play in which the manager of the Globe Theatre rebukes Shakespeare for creating a Jewish character and for conceiving Shylock as intolerantly as he did.

Among the recent writings of more noteworthy authors than those who have adventured with *The Merchant of Venice* in the past are John Cournos, St. John Ervine and Louis Untermeyer.

Shylock's Choice,[21] Cournos' one-act treatment, finds Shylock and

---

[16] Henry Duffy Traill, London, 1892.

[17] Oscar Fay Adams, Boston, 1903.

[18] F. Jackson, in *Shakespearean Quarterly*, Sydney, Australia, April, 1923.

[19] William Moses Blatt, in *After the Curtain Falls*, Boston, 1924.

[20] Tom J. Geraghty, in *Hollywood Plays*, edited by Kenyon Nicholson, New York, 1930.

[21] *Fortnightly Review*, vol. 124, London, 1925, p. 728ff.

Tubal in discussion on the evening preceding the trial. Shylock's intended revenge on Antonio is revealed in a different and more subtle form than that expressed in Shakespeare's play. He plans a strategy that will enable him, at the last minute, to fling away his knife, making the Christian indebted to Shylock for saving his life.

In *The Lady of Belmont*,[22] Ervine has developed the story with greater scope than any of his predecessors, and with the best results. His five-act play is a sequel to *The Merchant of Venice*. The scene is laid in the home of Portia and Bassanio, exactly ten years after the trial. The entire action takes place in less than twenty-four hours. Antonio clings tediously to a mistaken notion that the trial, a decade earlier, has made him a hero. The others have forgotten his act of friendship and are annoyed by his repeated references to his near-sacrifice. Bassanio, Gratiano and Lorenzo continue to be relentless Jew-baiters. Their wives find marriage an unhappy experience. Portia's fortune has been squandered by her philandering husband. She regrets the ruse by which she saved the merchant's life and damaged her uncle's reputation as a lawyer. Nerissa subjects her worthless husband to bitter tongue-lashings. Jessica, while despising her music-loving husband, willingly keeps from her children the knowledge of their despised Jewish ancestry. In an affair with Bassanio, she proves herself to be the same artful dissembler that she was when she eloped with Lorenzo. Shylock has recouped his wealth and although he enjoys the privilege of Christianity—he is now a Senator of Venice and a close friend of the Duke—he is secretly true to his Jewish faith. The years have mellowed him and when he and Portia meet, the two become mutually respectful in terms of the only intellectual integrity that is displayed by the characters of the play.

Ervine's play has enjoyed a number of revivals, possibly the most interesting of which was the one under Gilmor Brown's direction at the Pasadena Playhouse in 1941. If there was any virtue in featuring the continuity of the story, it was to be found on this occasion, when Brown who had appeared as Shylock in Shakespeare's play, was presented for the same audience the following month as Ervine's Jew.

---

[22] London, 1923.

Another modern treatment is Untermeyer's *The Merchant of Venice Act VI,* [23] which is developed differently from the earlier play of the same name. Six years after the trial, Shylock and Antonio are partners in business. Jessica has left Lorenzo and has returned to her father. Shylock remembers the trial as a mockery. He sees no essential distinction between Christians and Jews, and now that he has turned Christian, he attempts to persuade Tubal to follow his example. He sees all Christians, himself included, grasping for the material things of life.

The attempts to place Shylock in a musical setting have been generally unhappy. The earlier practice of loading the play with songs for Portia and her friends at least served to throw into relief the unmelodic Shylock scenes. The musical versions of *The Merchant of Venice* do not have this advantage. A number of Shakespeare's plays have been successfully adapted to opera, but these have not been for the edification of the lovers of Shakespeare. It is possible that in the hands of a competent composer, *The Merchant of Venice* can achieve status as a musical piece, but our concern here is not with the enrichment of operatic repertory, and in the two examples of musical experimentation with *The Merchant of Venice,* we find good reason for indifference. A burlesqued operatic version in five acts by Alice Gould[24] enjoyed no success whatever. The more serious effort of Adrian Beecham, son of Sir Thomas, was dismissed by London's *Daily Chronicle and Evening News* as an error in judgment. But his work, at least, utilized Shakespeare's actual text throughout, in a full operatic version. It saw production in 1921 and again the following year, but perhaps it remains the task of a more mature composer than the eighteen-year-old Beecham to effect the transformation successfully.

The motion-picture productions that recently presented Lawrence Olivier as Henry IV, Hamlet, and Richard III give us pause and are suggestive of the potentialities for presenting Shakespeare in this medium. They are a far cry from the sorry cinematic versions of *Romeo and Juliet* and *A Midsummer Night's Dream* of the 1930's and the 1912 motion picture version of *The Merchant of*

Venice (in two parts).[25] The last was announced as being "replete with gorgeous settings, faultless costuming and skillful acting," but it bears the unmistakable stamp of the circus. Publicity pictures disclose a be-turbaned, ill-looking Shylock, jubilant in the courtroom, grinning maliciously—his front teeth missing.

Not all the blame for desecrating Shakespeare's Shylock can be assigned to the tampering of second-rate authors. A fair share of the responsibility must be levelled at those actors who exploited the character only for the purpose of exhibiting their acting ability. Making Shylock grotesque was not limited to impersonations that portrayed him as ridiculous in appearance, speech and gesture. Imitating cripples on the stage was once a means of provoking mirth and a limping Shylock could be as supposedly comical as any other dramatic character with a physical handicap. *The Merchant of Venice* has been one of the most frequently used vehicles for debuts, and for many who tried the role of Shylock, the role was, unfortunately, trying. These were the "also-rans" of the theatre—the would-be professionals who did not possess the special alchemy that makes a good actor. In order to sublimate frustrated stage ambitions, many of them became the dramatic readers and elocutionists whose "one-man shows" usually featured Shylock on the program. The way in which an actor played Shylock was often the test of his virtuosity. Spectators had grown so familiar with all of the nuances of the Shylock role that they were able to appraise an actor's reading with some degree of expertness. Programs that displayed elocutionary talent were not generally regarded as first-rate "theatre," but the persistence of this form of entertainment over a long period bears clear witness to its popularity.

Possibly the most distorted images of Shylock were the ones undertaken by those performers who were least equipped to represent him—the women and children who, for reasons that could never have seemed sensible, appeared as Shakespeare's Jew. Doubtless, in the lists of "worsts" their names must appear first. One of the earliest male impersonators of Shylock was Clara Fisher, who, for over a full decade, achieved popularity in England and America. She had been hailed at the Drury Lane as a prodigy at the age

---

[25] A Kleine-Eclipse Feature Film.

CATHERINE MACREADY as SHYLOCK
Brander Matthews Dramatic Museum, Columbia University

of six; when she was sixteen, her reputation as an actress was assured in New York. During the 1820's, she elicited repeated commendations for her acting of Shylock, and the critics praised her for what they found to be a fresh, charming and captivating manner.

Charlotte Cushman, one of the most celebrated American actresses of the nineteenth century, found a favorite role in Shylock in the 1860's. Miss Cushman had played Portia to Macready's and Edwin Booth's Shylocks, but this did not deter her from attempting the more exacting role. Her familiarity with masculine parts dated back to the 1830's, when her acting of Romeo had been acclaimed, and she probably sought in Shylock a character that was better suited to her maturity.

A decade later, the somewhat masculine Mrs. Catherine Macready, wife of the acclaimed actor, assumed the Shylock role on both sides of the Atlantic but it is difficult to assess the effectiveness of this dramatic curio.

A more recent female Shylock was Lucille La Verne, who presented her impersonation in London in 1929. The actress had gained a reputation for her portrayal of Widow Cagle in *Sun-Up*, and she felt confident that her Shylock would please. The critics refused to take her venture seriously. The writer on *The London Times* found her manner reminiscent of Sir Harry Lauder; he apparently enjoyed her performance: ". . . it makes more noise than most; this Shylock occasionally left the Rialto; never the Contralto."[26]

It was in the faltering steps and high-pitched tones of child-actors that the long-suffering Shylock received his most incongruous treatment. Weaning infant actors on Shakespeare must have been a traumatic experience for the children at least, for most of them were never heard from again in the theatre. When eleven-year-old Master Burke portrayed Shylock in New York, *The Mirror*, while praising him most for his rich and natural brogue, called his Shakespearean venture unsuccessful, although it admitted that it was his naiveté that afforded the greatest pleasure. Unlike Edmund Kean's pre-adolescent experience with Shylock, young Burke's career seems to have terminated at this point.

---

[26] Quoted in *Literary Digest*, October 26, 1929.

The middle years of the nineteenth century, particularly in America, saw a considerable number of infant prodigies on the stage. Among the youthful Shylocks were Jean M. Davenport, an aspiring male impersonator, and a Master Reeder, whose Shylock could be seen at new bargain rates of 37½¢ and 12½¢. They, too, seem to have run their brief course with this one effort. Sister-acts enjoyed a brief vogue. Lora Gordon Boon and Anna Isabella Boon appeared in several two-week engagements and included with their Shylock and Portia scene, other ambitious bits of *Macbeth, King Lear, Julius Caesar, Hamlet* and *Romeo and Juliet.* They were tolerated and even encouraged; only such a later recorder as Odell referred to these child-performers as "little pests."

The most precocious of the babies were Kate and Ellen Bateman. Ellen was four years old and Kate's Portia was all of six. If we shudder at the lisping quality of the nursery courtroom, we must at least admit our amazement at the memory feat that enabled Ellen to portray, in addition to her Shylock, a knee-high Richard and a diminutive Lady Macbeth, while her older sister presented a not much more mature Richmond and Macbeth. Their programs were in great demand at first-run houses as well as in the lecture halls. Kate Bateman was the exception to the rule that found most of these children professionals "played out" by the time they had reached their teens; she later became a distinguished actress.

The apprenticeship system instituted by Macklin's school for student actors in the eighteenth century had little bearing on actual theatrical experience for stage aspirants. Nevertheless it developed, in time, into a large and lucrative business. Evidence of its growth can be seen in the dramatic schools that flourish in our large cities, but their success in providing stage-struck students with opportunities in the professional theatre is no greater than it was in 1750. The scores of untalented actors who fell by the wayside, but who were not content to stay there, crowded the stage with generations of performers who refused to be discouraged. The professional status of actors was not always as zealously guarded as it is today. On special occasions, and doubtless for a consideration, it was possible for an amateur to appear in a leading role, supported by a cast of seasoned players. Numerous play-bills have listed as Shylock "a gentleman who has never before appeared on any stage," often concealing the name of the novice. One of the most celebrated amateur actors was George Henry Lewes, whose appreciation of the theatre outstripped his acting ability. His appearance as Shylock in an Edinburgh production in 1849 was regarded with great interest, but it is as a critic that he made his mark.

Charles Kean's era fathered the largest number of "elocutionists." Teachers of diction, schools of expression, programs of readings, were the order of the day. Auditoriums, museums, concert and lecture halls were engaged for recitals in and out of season, featuring "professors," amateurs, second-rate and indigent actors, both in and out of costume. Their audiences were largely the members of women's clubs, who were apparently eager to attend such programs in the morning, afternoon or evening. Such readers as H. J. Finn and John W. S. Hows were the chief recipients of the applause, and their programs, including *The Merchant of Venice,* varied little from season to season. *The Mirror,* on one occasion, called Finn's interpretation of the trial scene "broadly ludicrous," but this criticism seemed to disturb neither him nor his audience and his return engagements multiplied. Hows, who edited *The Shakespearean Reader,*[27] and was professor of elocution at Columbia College, occasionally rewarded his listeners with a recital of Poe's *The Bells,* following his reading of *The Merchant of Venice.*

Fanny Kemble, in her later years, maintained herself by appearing in programs of readings adapted from classical plays. *The Merchant of Venice* was one of her favorites. A host of "soloists" became popular through benefit performances for charity organizations and the outstanding actors of the day followed this trend. Henry Irving and Ellen Terry frequently responded to benefit appeals with their rendition of the trial scene, contrary though the practice was to Irving's initial theory of the play's unity in its five-act presentation. Many of these elocutionists displayed, evidently, great feats of memory. During the 1860's, one of the busiest elocutionists was Professor Fitzgerald Tasistro, who was billed as "the man who can render his selections without book or prompter." When Irving's career was at its peak, Professor Locke Richardson of Syracuse University toured the large cities with a program that consisted solely of a recitation of *The Merchant of*

---

[27] New York, 1849.

Venice. For more than a decade, he appeared in annual recitals in New York and enlisted the support of a group of enthusiastic followers. Robert Raikes Raymond and Sidney Woollett were other elocutionists who were widely known during this period for their recitals of *The Merchant of Venice* from memory. Raymond's edition of Shakespeare's plays[28] demonstrates his method of foreshortening the original works. For most of these declaimers, characterization was not very important.

When America was frontier land, Noah Ludlow, transported by wagon and flatboats to the farthest outposts of the country with Drake's Travelling Players, presented a tobacco-chewing comic version of Shakespeare's play. Two decades later, with part of the company still intact, the troupe appeared in Milledgeville, Georgia, in a performance of *The Merchant of Venice* because the legislature was in session there. Twenty years more, and the country had not grown too sophisticated to enjoy a travesty on the play. A burlesque version of *The Merchant of Venice* by Griffin and Christy's Minstrels in California was a favorite program of the Gold Rush days.

We must not attribute solely to the primitive culture of the smaller towns in early America the enjoyment of caricature. Centuries of artistic development in England found its playgoers equally appreciative of parody. When a Negro actor, billed as the African Roscius, appeared in a program as Oroonoko, or the Royal Slave, as singer of *Opossum Up A Tree* and as Shylock in the trial scene, the incongruity was not as apparent as its entertainment value.

George Jones built a dubious theatrical reputation on his ability to keep audiences in a state of tumult that was mistaken for hilarity. There was nothing particularly noteworthy in his early career as an interpreter of legitimate drama, and seeking about for some means of rousing his public, he hit upon the notion of calling in the police in order to create excitement. He soon became a favorite with rowdy college boys who attended his performances for the sole purpose of forcibly presenting him with vegetables. His *Hamlet, Romeo and Juliet* and *The Merchant of Venice* met with equal insult. New Yorkers in the 1870's came to know him as Count Joannes, "the Great Uncrushed."

Others began to capitalize on burlesquing Shakespeare and the

---

[28] *Shakespeare for the Young Folk,* New York, 1881.

late 1880's found Count Joannes sharing jeers with several rivals. James Owen O'Connor was one of these imitators. He usually could be depended on to include *The Merchant of Venice*. The *Herald* called his Shylock "too contemptible to be noticed in these columns."[29] Such buffoonery was not relegated only to the less important houses. O'Connor held forth at the Star Theatre, where Irving had but recently appeared as Shylock. Hamlet, Richard III and Richelieu were other victims of his heavy-handed treatment. The rumor that he was probably mentally unsound did not deter his audiences from enjoying his vulgar performances.

Ira H. Moore was another contender for these questionable honors. His choice of program was more selective but equally successful. The trial scene was sandwiched in with other favorites of the day that included such selections as *Mixed Pickles, For Congress* and *The Two Orphans*.

Equally incongruous are the revivals that featured great foreign actors speaking Shylock's lines in their native tongues while the supporting casts read Shakespeare's lines in the original. Notable among such performances was that of Jacob Adler, the idol of the Yiddish theatre, who spoke in Yiddish with an English-speaking company.

The custom of loading the play with "extras," as did Charles Kean, Tree, and Sothern, has been described elsewhere, but when characters are included which deter the action of the play, the practice must be considered excessive. In the days of the Federal Theatre Project of the Works Progress Administration, the cast for *The Merchant of Venice* added four clowns "of the Commedia dell' Arte," a boy, a friend of Antonio, a Christian and a singer, among others. But if we are too critical of this crowding of the play, we must recall that Shakespeare was being exploited here, more or less practically, as a means of creating employment.

When Ian Keith and Estelle Winwood played the leads in *The Merchant of Venice* in Minneapolis, the program boasted thirty-five Jews and sixty Christians. In vain had Granville-Barker complained about the custom of surrounding Shylock with a small crowd of sympathetic Jews. This production featured a red-wigged Shylock and an explanatory note concerning recent findings of Professor Thomas Marc Parrot that unearthed the origin of Shakespeare's

[29] April 12, 1888.

source for Shylock. The pound of flesh story was not taken from old Roman fables, according to the current newspaper accounts. It was in the satiric verse of a contemporary Italian poet, Aretino, that Shakespeare had found reference to the red-haired Jew. The late Professor Parrott was not aware of the fact that his name had been taken in vain. He was equally innocent of having discovered any such source for Shylock.

The public and the press were entreated not to divulge the "original" ending of the play. The publicity for this production read:

> It commits the sin of adding one word that Shakespeare never wrote; it is justified we trust, in that it knits the entire theme of the play into a final ironic comment.

The secret was zealously guarded; no account in the press divulges the keyword. Estelle Winwood later recalled that the word was "sign." With monotonous insistence, the Christians in the courtroom pointed to Shylock and chorused the word repeatedly, until a hypnotized Shylock finally signed away his adherence to Judaism. He was not really a villain; it was the Christians who were the heartless ones.

The custom of presenting Shakespeare's plays in modern dress is not new. Garrick's productions were costumed in contemporary clothes, and although the span of years from Elizabethan to Restoration drama was not great, the effect must have seemed as anachronistic to any purists in the audience as do such adaptations today. Rationalizing a modern setting for a Shakespearean play takes one of several forms. If it is experimental, the reason that is usually given for the venture is that the production is motivated by the best intentions to make the play live in the here and now. Amateurs, who often experiment with Shakespeare in modern dress, can afford the indulgence of candidly confessing their limitations in undertaking the pageantry of historically accurate mounting. Most "modern-dress" productions rest on the somewhat apologetic application of the thought that Shakespeare was not of an age, but for all time. Cardozo has called the play "a medley of primitive data incapable of consistent and convincing modernization . . . it should be read in the spirit of . . . pure fiction."

Perhaps it is in this spirit that Michael Langham's Stratford-on-Avon production experimented with costuming the play in eighteenth century dress. The reviewer for *Punch* (April 27, 1960) saw nothing extraordinary in this mounting of *The Merchant of Venice*. He called it simple and intelligent and praised it for its unostentatious sets. The company was shown off admirably in the period attire. He found Peter O'Toole's Shylock refreshing; not the character of the traditionally cringing stage-Jew, but a fiercely independent fellow.

> . . . His courtesy is impeccable, his resolution steely; the result is extremely impressive, and against the appalling arrogance of Antonio and his caddish hangers-on he appears to be almost the only gentleman in Venice.

With *The Merchant of Venice* there is the special temptation to distort the play into a campaign of special pleading for the Jew, and the resources of the costume department are often used to further such designs. Program notes for such productions usually become suspiciously eloquent in their effort to affirm their adherence to the spirit of Shakespeare. There are varying degrees of fidelity to the text, but such versions, in most cases, leave the impression of being no more than stunts. There is a world of intentional difference between Granville's versions that did their worst by Shakespeare and more recent stage presentations that masquerade as Shakespearean. Both produce the same incongruous effect.

An ambitious New York production of *The Merchant of Venice* severely taxed the tolerance of the playgoer. Act I featured Elizabethan costumes, a clowning red-wigged Shylock; Act II was set in eighteenth century age-of-enlightenment Germany, with powdered wigs and brocades, while the concluding act found Shylock the victim of Nazis in a concentration camp.[30] The result, one must report, was a fiasco. The same may be said of a five-act modern-dress version of the play in which Shakespeare's lines were left intact and a program note credited Hammacher-Schlemmer with furnishing a tea-wagon.[31]

If these attempts to present Shylock were, in reality, profanations of Shakespeare's work, most of them were unintentionally so and were based on an ignorance of the spirit and the traditions of the play. In any case, they present a sad summary of the miscellaneous efforts to dramatize Shakespeare's Jew.

[30] A Pargod production in Hebrew, November, 1948, in New York.
[31] Stead Collection.

EPILOGUE

". . . either for tragedy, comedy, history . . ."

The character of Shylock, more than any other that Shakespeare created, is at the mercy of the actor who portrays it. The quality of Shylock's personality has long been an enigma to those who have attempted to understand it. Had Shakespeare intended to make an out-and-out villain of his Jew, he would not have endowed him with sensitivities that draw upon our humanitarian instincts. Conversely, had he aimed at enlisting our sympathies for a pathetic Shylock, he would not have so infused him with evil. A monstrous Shylock, without any human overtones would, doubtless, have pleased the Elizabethans; but Shakespeare's genius went beyond his era. It is questionable whether Shylock's career as a stage-Jew would have lasted any longer than that of Barabas, had Shakespeare made him less complex. It is in this very complexity that actors have found inspiration. Comedians and tragedians have been equally rewarded in the role.

At no time, no matter how effectively he comes to life on the stage, can we say with certainty that *this* is the Jew that Shakespeare drew. If Shylock takes on human form, he must act as human beings act. He changes; he grows; he is subject to the moods of the other real people of his sixteenth century Venice or London. In short, he is organic. We cannot see his figure, now in miniature, now blown up to mammoth proportions. He is life-size. He is neither the aristocratic Jew of Arliss' characterization, nor the clowning puppet of Doggett. He is the Shylock of any actor who can make him come to life within the environment of the play itself.

Poel, on the one hand, advocated that only by reproducing the unadorned quality of Elizabethan staging, can we recapture Shakespeare's meaning. Ivor Brown is more liberal. He accords to the producer all the leeway the stage can offer, from Poel's "bare-bones" presentation to the most elaborate setting that can be dreamed up: "if you can do it well and in its own kind." In other words, if time and space can be made to adhere; if the director can be firm of purpose in envisioning a production where neither actor, nor staging, nor script will unmake him, but will combine to reflect the magnificent wholeness of Shakespeare, he will then be true to his professional calling.

Is it captious to reason that we can appreciate Shakespeare only when we bring to the theatre the inevitable baggage of present-day thinking? When society has progressed to that point where it can consider itself released from the strangle-hold of its anti-social attitudes, it will be better able to comprehend the evil from which it emerged and the factors that motivated that evil. An understanding of the Elizabethan state of mind is more readily approached when we attempt to view it in retrospect. We do not do violence to the spirit of Shakespeare when we attempt to translate him into our contemporary modes. A Bach score is no less musically sound because it is played on a piano instead of a harpsichord. A play that is staged with Elizabethan accuracy, as Poel attempted to do, can be an aesthetic delight, but its antique quality does not make it very durable for long use. It would seem, then, that only in a production that is based on sound Shakespearean tradition can there be an opportunity in our day for clarifying Shylock on the stage.

Hamlet, according to Linton's study, was the most frequently acted Shakespeare play in London from Irving's day to recent times. It has already been pointed out that *The Merchant of Venice* came next in the number of revivals. *Twelfth Night* was third, but it was placed in this position only because of Beerbohm Tree's numerous revivals. *Romeo and Juliet,* surprisingly, was only eighth in popularity. We cannot, however, overlook the fact that it was more a matter of finding in Shylock a rewarding role, than any conviction about the significance of the play itself, that made the great actors of the past turn to it again and again. Of course, it may have been more than fortuitous that the changing social scene continued to give a certain contemporaneous and topical interest to Shakespeare's Jew.

In studying the development of the role of Shylock through the years, one becomes increasingly conscious of the changing face of the character and of the audience that viewed it. In Shakespeare's Shylock, Elizabethan theatre-goers were able to find a personality that conformed with their preconceptions of the villainy of the Jews. Seventeenth-century audiences responded readily to the ludicrous quality that their Shylock actors emphasized. Macklin's public was startled into taking his Shylock seriously. Spectators discovered a credible Jew in Edmund Kean's portrayal. Edwin Booth displayed facets in the role that further humanized it. The Victorians sought and found social motivations for the sympathetic interpretation that Irving gave to Shylock. In our own day Shylock has served the individual talents of the actors who have played him. He emerges, finally, as a superb theatrical character, whose creator possessed the astonishing genius that was able through the ages

> To show Virtue her own feature, Scorn her own image, and the very age and body of the time his form and pressure.

BIBLIOGRAPHY

Adams, Oscar Fay, *The Merchant of Venice, Act VI*, Boston, Cornhill Booklet, 1903.

Adams, William Davenport, *A Dictionary of the Drama*, London, Chatto and Windus, 1904.

Adler, Elkan Nathan, *London*, Philadelphia, Jewish Publication Society of America, 1930.

(Anonymous), *The (Old Clothes) Merchant of Venice; or The Young Judge and Old Jewry*, New York, Dewitt, 1884.

Anthony, Gordon, *John Gielgud*, London, Geoffrey Bles, 1938.

Ausubel, Nathan, Editor, *A Treasury of Jewish Folklore*, New York, Crown Publishers, 1948.

Baker, D. E., et. al., *Biographia Dramatica*, London, 1812.

Baker, George Melville, *The Peddler of Very Nice*, Boston, Lee and Sheppard, W. V. Spencer, 1866.

Baker, H. Barton, *The London Stage: Its History and Traditions from 1576 to 1888*, London, W. H. Allen and Company, 1889.

Baron, Salo Wittmayer, *A Social and Religious History of the Jews*, 3 vols., Columbia University Press, 1937.

————, *The Jewish Community—Its History and Structure to the American Revolution*, Philadelphia, Jewish Publication Society of America, Vol. I, 1942.

Beerbohm, Max, *Around Theatres*, Vol. II, New York, Alfred A. Knopf, 1930.

————, *Herbert Beerbohm Tree*, London, Hutchinson and Company, (n.d.).

Bernard, John, *Retrospections of the Stage*, 2 vols., London, Henry Colburn and Richard Bentley, 1830.

Besant, Sir Walter, *London in the Eighteenth Century*, London, Adam and Charles Black, 1903.

Blatt, William Mosher, "The Quality of Mercy," *After the Curtain Rises*, Boston, W. H. Baker and Company, 1924.

Boaden, James, *Memoirs of the Life of John Philip Kemble*, Vol. I, London, Longman, Hurst, Rees, Orme, Brown and Green, 1825.

Bourchier, Arthur, *Some Reflections on the Drama and Shakespeare*, Oxford, B. H. Blackwell, 1911.

Bradbrook, Muriel Clara, *Themes and Conventions of Elizabethan Tragedy,* Cambridge, University Press, 1935.

Brereton, Austin, *The Lyceum Theatre and Henry Irving,* London, Lawrence and Bullen, (n.d.).

——, *The Life of Henry Irving,* 2 vols., London, Longmans, Green and Company, 1908.

Brougham, John, *Much Ado About A Merchant of Venice,* New York, Samuel French, 1868.

Brown, Ivor, *Shakespeare,* Garden City, Doubleday and Company, Inc., 1949.

Brown, T. Allston, *A History of the New York Stage,* 3 vols., New York, Dodd, Mead and Company, 1903.

Cardoza, J. L., *The Contemporary Jew in Elizabethan Drama,* Amsterdam, H. J. Paris, 1925.

Chambers, Edmund K., *The Elizabethan Stage,* Oxford, Clarendon Press, 1923.

Chapman, John Kemble, editor, *A Complete History of Theatrical Entertainments,* London, John Mitchell, 1849 (?).

Churchill, Charles, *The Rosciad,* London, printed for the author, 1763.

Cibber, Colley, *An Apology for His Life,* London, J. M. Dent and Sons, Ltd., 1938.

Cole, John William, *The Life and Theatrical Times of Charles Kean,* 2 vols., London, Richard Bentley, 1859.

Coleman, Edward D., *The Jew in English Drama,* New York, New York Public Library, 1943.

Collier, John Payne, *Illustrations of Old English Literature,* Vol. III, London, privately printed, 1866.

Cook, Dutton, *A Book of the Play,* 2 vols., London, Samson Low, Marston, Searle and Rivington, 1876.

——, *Hours with The Players,* London, Chatto and Windus, 1881.

——, *On the Stage,* London, Sampson Low, Marston, Searle and Rivington, 1883.

Cooke, William, *Memoirs of Charles Macklin, Comedian,* London, Jones Asperne, 1806.

Cournos, John, "Shylock's Choice," London, *Fortnightly Review,* Vol. 124, 1925.

Craig, Edward Gordon, *Henry Irving,* London, J. M. Dent and Sons, Ltd., 1930.

Cumberland, Richard, *Memoirs,* London, Lackington, Allen and Company, 1806.

Daly, Frederick, *Henry Irving in England and America,* New York, R. Worthington, 1884.

Davies, Thomas, *Dramatic Miscellanies,* Vol. II, Dublin, 1784.

——————, *Memoirs of the Life of David Garrick,* London, printed for the author, 1780.

Donne, William Bodham, *Essays on the Drama,* London, John W. Parker and Son, 1858.

Doran, John, *"Their Majesties' Servants." Annals of the English Stage,* Vol. II, New York, W. J. Widdleton, 1865.

Downes, John, *Roscius Anglicanus,* London, printed for the editor, 1789.

Duggan, G. C., *The Stage Irishman,* Dublin, Talbot Press, 1939.

Dunlap, William, *A History of the American Theatre,* New York, J. and J. Harper, 1832.

Dunn, Esther Cloudman, *Shakespeare in America,* New York, Macmillan Company, 1939.

Engel, M., *Practical Illustrations of Rhetorical Gesture and Action,* adapted to the English Drama by Henry Siddons, London, 1807.

Ervine, St. John G., *The Lady of Belmont,* London, G. Allen and Unwin, Ltd., 1923.

Fitzgerald, Percy, *The Life of David Garrick,* Vol. I, London, Tinsley Bros., 1868.

Fleay, Frederick Gard, *A Chronicle History of the London Stage,* New York, G. E. Stechert, 1909.

Fraser, Frederick John, *The Merry Merchant of Venice,* Allahabad, 1895.

Gardiner, William, *The Music of Nature,* Boston, Oliver Ditson and Company, 1837.

Garrick's receipt books, Mss., Folger Shakespeare Library.

Genest, John, *Some Account of the English Stage from the Restoration in 1660 to 1830,* 10 vols., Bath, H. E. Carrington, 1830.

Gentleman, Francis, *Dramatic Censor: or Critical Companion,* Vol. I, London, J. Bell and C. Etherington, 1770.

Geraghty, Tom J., *"A Pound of Flesh," Hollywood Plays,* edited by Kenyon Nicholson, 1930, New York.

Gielgud, John, *Easy Stages,* New York, Macmillan Company, 1939.

Gould, Alice, *The Merchant of Venice,* Boston, W. H. Baker Company, 1929.

Gould, Thomas R., *The Tragedian,* New York, Hurd and Houghton, 1868.

Granville-Barker, Harley and Harrison, G. B., *A Companion to Shakespeare Studies,* New York, Macmillan Company, 1936.

Granville-Barker, Harley, *Prefaces to Shakespeare,* Princeton, Princeton University Press, 1946.

——————, *Associating with Shakespeare,* London, Oxford University Press, 1932.

Gray, C. H., *Theatrical Criticism in London to 1795,* New York, Columbia University Press, 1931.

Harbage, Alfred, *Annals of the English Drama 975-1700*, Philadelphia, University of Pennsylvania Press, 1940.

————, "Elizabethan Acting," New York, *Publication of Modern Language Association*, Vol. LIV, No. 3, 1939.

Harrison, G. B., *An Elizabethan Journal*, New York, Cosmopolitan Book Corp., 1929.

————, *Shakespeare Under Elizabeth*, New York, Henry Holt and Company, 1933.

Hawkins, Frederick W., *The Life of Edmund Kean*, 2 vols., London, Tinsley Bros., 1869.

Hazlitt, William, *Characters of Shakespeare's Plays*, New York, Wiley and Putnam, 1845.

Henslowe, Philip, *Diary from 1591 to 1609*, edited by John Payne Collier, London, Shakespeare Society, 1845.

Hill, Sir John, *The Actor: or a Treatise on the Art of Playing*, London, R. Griffiths, (n.d.).

Hillebrand, Harold Newcomb, *Edmund Kean*, New York, Columbia University Press, 1933.

Hitchcock, Robert, *An Historical View of the Irish Stage*, Vols. I and II, Dublin, R. Marchbank.

Hogan, Charles Beecher, *Shakespeare in the Theatre, 1701-1800. A Record of Performances in London 1701-1750*, Oxford, Clarendon Press, 1952.

Horne, Richard Henigst, "A Dramatic Reverie," Furness *New Variorum The Merchant of Venice*, Philadelphia, J. B. Lippincott, 1895.

Hows, John W. S., *The Shakespearean Reader*, New York, D. Appleton and Company, 1849.

Hunt, John, *Critical Essays of the Performers of the London Theatres*, London, 1807.

Hunt, Leigh, *Autobiography*, Vol. I, New York, Harper and Bros., 1850.

Ibn-Sahav, Ari, *Jessica, My Daughter*, New York, Crown Publishers, 1948.

Irving, Henry, *Impressions of America*, Vol. I, edited by Joseph Hatton, London, Sampson, Low, Marston, Searle and Rivington, 1884.

Jackson, F., "Shylock Returns," Sidney, Australia, Shakespearean Quarterly, April, 1923.

Jacobs, Joseph, *Jews of Angevin England*, London, G. P. Putnam's Sons, 1893.

James, Henry, *The Scenic Art—Notes on Acting and the Drama, 1872-1901*, New Brunswick, Rutgers University Press, 1948.

Jordan, Thomas, "The Forfeiture," *Royal Arbor of Loyal Poesie*, London, 1664.

Kirkman, James Thomas, *Memoirs of the Life of Charles Macklin*, 2 vols., London, Lackington, Allen and Company, 1799.

Knight, Joseph, *Theatrical Notes,* London, Lawrence and Bullen, 1893.

Larks, The (pseudo.), *The Shakespeare Water-Cure,* New York, Roorbach and Company, 1883.

Landa, Myer Jack, *The Jew in Drama,* London, P. S. King and Son Ltd., 1926.

————, *The Shylock Myth,* London, W. H. Allen and Company, Ltd., 1942.

Lewes, George Henry, *On Actors and the Art of Acting,* New York, Henry Holt and Company, 1878.

Lewisohn, Ludwig, *The Last Days of Shylock,* New York, Harper and Bros., 1931.

Lichtenberg, Georg Christoph, *Vermischte Schriften,* Vol. III, Goettingen, 1867.

Linton, Calvin Darlington, *Shakespearean Staging in London from Irving to Gielgud,* Baltimore, Johns Hopkins University, 1940.

MacMillan, Dougald, compiler, *Drury Lane Calendar 1747-1776,* Oxford, Clarendon Press, 1938.

Malone, Edmond, *An Historical Account of the English Stage,* London, S. and E. Harding, 1793.

Margolis, Max L. and Marx, Alexander, *A History of the Jewish People,* Philadelphia, Jewish Publication Society of America, 1927.

Marston, Westland, *Our Recent Actors,* Boston, Robert Bros., 1888.

Martin, Sir John, *Autobiography,* London, Harvey Sampson Low, Marston and Company, 1933.

Matthews, Brander, *Playwrights on Playmaking,* New York, Charles Scribners' Sons, 1923.

Matthews, Brander and Hutton, Lawrence, *Actors and Actresses of Great Britain and the United States,* New York, Cassell and Company, Ltd., 1886.

————, editors, *David Garrick and his Contemporaries,* Boston, L. C. Page and Company, 1886.

Miner, Carl S. and others, *The Merchant of Venice,* Cedar Rapids, Iowa, Record Printing Company, 1896 (?).

Modder, Montagu Frank, *The Jew in the Literature of England,* Philadelphia, Jewish Publication Society of America, 1939.

Molloy, Joseph Fitzgerald, *The Life and Adventures of Edmund Kean,* London, Downey and Company, 1897.

Moses, Montrose J., *The American Dramatist,* Boston, Little, Brown, and Company, 1925.

Murdock, James, *The Stage,* Philadelphia, J. M. Stoddert, 1880.

Nicoll, Allardyce, *A History of Restoration Drama, 1660-1700,* Cambridge, University Press, 1928.

————, *A History of Early Eighteenth Century Drama, 1700-1750,* Cambridge, University Press, 1925.

————, *A History of Late Eighteenth Century Drama, 1750-1800,* Cambridge, University Press, 1927.

————, *The Development of the Theatre,* New York, Harcourt, Brace and Company, 1937.

Odell, George C. D., *Shakespeare from* Betterton to Irving, 2 vols., New York, Charles Scribners' Sons, 1920.

————, *Annals of the New York Stage,* vols. I-XIV, New York, Columbia University Press, 1927-1945.

Parry, Edward Abbott, *Charles Macklin,* London, Kegan Paul, Trench, Trubner and Company, Ltd., 1891.

Pepys, Samuel, *Diary,* London, J. M. Dent and Sons, Ltd., 1943.

Plain, Timothy, *Letters Respecting Performances at the Theatre-Royal,* Edinburgh, G. Gray, 1800.

Poel, William, *Shakespeare in the Theatre,* London, Sidgwick and Jackson, Ltd., 1913.

Pollock, Sir Frederick, *Macready's Reminiscences,* New York, Harper and Bros., 1875.

Proctor, B. W., *The Life of Edmund Kean,* 2 vols., London, Edward Moxon, 1835.

Quinn, Arthur Hobson, *A History of the American Drama, From the Beginning to the Civil War,* New York, Harper and Brothers, 1923.

Ralli, Augustus John, *A History of Shakespearean Criticism,* London, Oxford University Press, 1932.

Raymond, Robert Raikes, *Shakespeare for the Young Folk,* New York, Fords, Howard and Hulbert, 1881.

Roach, John, *Authentic Memoirs of the Green Room, for 1801,* London, 1801.

Robinson, Herbert Spenser, *English Shakespearean Criticism in the Eighteenth Century,* New York, H. W. Wilson Company, 1932.

Roth, Cecil, *A Bird's Eye View of Jewish History,* Cincinnati, Union of American Hebrew Congregations, 1935.

————, "The Background of Shylock," *The Review of English Studies,* Vol. IX, No. 34, April, 1933.

————, *A Life of Menasseh Ben Israel,* Philadelphia, Jewish Publication Society of America, 1934.

Rowe, Nicholas, "Some Account of the Life of Mr. William Shakespeare," *Shakespeare Criticism,* D. Nichol Smith, Editor, London, Oxford University Press, 1930.

Saintsbury, H. A. and Cecil Palmer, editors, *We Saw Him Act,* London, Hurst and Blackett, 1939.

Shakespeare, William, *The Merchant of Venice*, London, J. Roberts, 1600.

————, *The Merchant of Venice*, London, Bell's edition, 1774 and 1775.

————, *The Merchant of Venice*, revised by J. P. Kemble, London, C. Lowndes, 1797.

————, *The Merchant of Venice*, J. Roach's edition, London, 1804.

————, *The Merchant of Venice*, revised by J. P. Kemble, London, John Miller, 1814.

————, *The Merchant of Venice*, W. Oxberry edition, London, W. Simkin and R. Marshall, 1820.

————, *The Merchant of Venice*, Charles Kean's Prompt-book, Drury Lane, November, 1846 performance, Folger Shakespeare Library.

————, *The Merchant of Venice*, Charles Kean edition, London, J. K. Chapman and Company, 1858.

————, *The Merchant of Venice*, Edwin Booth edition, notes by Henry L. Hinton, New York, C. A. Alvord, 1867.

————, *The Merchant of Venice*, Edwin Booth prompt-book, Folger Shakespeare Library.

————, *The Merchant of Venice*, edited by Henry Irving, London, Chiswick Press, 1879.

————, *The Merchant of Venice*, special Irving edition, London, Chiswick Press, 1880.

————, *The Merchant of Venice*, Henry Irving and Frank A. Marshall, editors, Vol. III, New York, Scribner and Welford, 1890.

————, *The Merchant of Venice*, Henry Irving prompt-book, Folger Shakespeare Library.

————, *The Merchant of Venice*, Horace Howard Furness New Variorum edition, Philadelphia, J. B. Lippincott Company, 1895.

————, *The Merchant of Venice*, Arthur Bourchier edition, London, Ballantyne Press, 1905.

————, *The Merchant of Venice*, Sir Herbert Beerbohm Tree prompt-book, Folger Shakespeare Library.

————, *The Merchant of Venice*, E. H. Sothern prompt-book, Folger Shakespeare Library.

————, *The Merchant of Venice*, David Belasco edition, New York, privately printed, 1922.

Short, Ernest, *Theatrical Cavalcade*, London, Eyre and Spottiswoode, 1942.

Sinsheimer, Hermann, *Shylock, The History of a Character or the Myth of the Jew*, London, Victor Gollancz, Ltd., 1947.

Small, Samuel Asa, *Shakespearean Character Interpretation: The Merchant of Venice*, Goettingen, Vandenhoed and Ruprecht, 1927.

Sprague, Arthur Colby, *Shakespeare and the Actors*, Cambridge, Harvard University Press, 1945.

Stoker, Bram, *Personal Reminiscences of Henry Irving*, 2 vols., London, William Heineman, 1906.

Stoll, Elmer Edgar, "Shakespeare's Jew," *University of Toronto Quarterly*, January 1939.

————, "Shylock," *Journal of English and German Philology*, Vol. X, No. 2, 1911.

Stone, George Winchester, Jr., *Garrick's Treatment of Shakespeare's Plays and his Influence upon the Changed Attitude of Shakespearean Criticism during the Eighteenth Century*, unpublished Harvard doctoral dissertation, 1940.

Symmonds, H. D., *The Secret History of the Green Room*, London, 1792.

Talfourd, Francis N., *Shylock: or The Merchant of Venice Preserved*, London, T. H. Lacy, 185?.

Tannenbaum, Samuel A., *Shakespeare's The Merchant of Venice. A Concise Bibliography*, New York, Samuel A. Tannenbaum, 1941.

Terry, Ellen, *The Story of My Life*, London, Hutchinson and Company, 1908.

Thaler, Alwin, *Shakespeare to Sheridan*, Cambridge, Harvard Press, 1922.

Towse, John Ranken, *Sixty Years of the Theatre*, New York, Funk and Wagnalls Company, 1916.

Toynbee, William Barr, editor, *The Diaries of William Charles Macready*, 2 vols., London, Chapman and Hall, Ltd., 1912.

Traill, Henry Duffy, "The Third Age," *Number Twenty: Fables and Fantasies*, London, 1892.

Untermeyer, Louis, "The Merchant of Venice Act VI," *Selected Poems and Parodies*, New York, 1935.

van der Veen, H. R. S., *Jewish Characters in Eighteenth Century English Fiction and Drama*, Groningen, 1935.

Vickers, George Morely, *Petruchio's Widow*, Philadelphia, Ideal Entertainments, 1888.

Warren, Edward H., *Shakespeare in Wall Street*, Boston, Houghton Mifflin Company, 1929.

Webster, Margaret, *Shakespeare Without Tears*, New York, Whittlesey House, 1942.

Wilson, J. Dover, *The Essential Shakespeare*, Cambridge, University Press, 1932.

Wilson, J. H., "Granville's 'stock-jobbing Jew'," *Philological Quarterly*, Vol. XIII, 1934.

Wilstach, Paul, *Richard Mansfield—The Man and the Actor*, New York, Charles Scribner's Sons, 1908.

Winter, William, *The Life and Art of Edwin Booth*, New York, Macmillan and Company, 1894.

————, *Shakespeare on the Stage,* First Series, New York, Moffat, Yard and Company, 1911. Second series, 1915.

————, *Shadows of the Stage,* New York, Macmillan and Company, 1892.

Wolf, Lucien, *Presidential Address,* Manchester, Jewish Historical Society of England, November 21, 1926.

Wolfe, Humbert, *Portraits by Inference,* London, Methuen and Company, Ltd., 1934.

Zangwill, Israel, "Shylock and Other Stage Jews," *The Voice of Jerusalem,* London, William Heinemann, 1920.

INDEX

147